AF450168

BOHEMIA
UNDER HAPSBURG MISRULE

LECTOR HOUSE PUBLIC DOMAIN WORKS

This book is a result of an effort made by Lector House towards making a contribution to the preservation and repair of original classic literature. The original text is in the public domain in the United States of America, and possibly other countries depending upon their specific copyright laws.

In an attempt to preserve, improve and recreate the original content, certain conventional norms with regard to typographical mistakes, hyphenations, punctuations and/or other related subject matters, have been corrected upon our consideration. However, few such imperfections might not have been rectified as they were inherited and preserved from the original content to maintain the authenticity and construct, relevant to the work. The work might contain a few prior copyright references as well as page references which have been retained, wherever considered relevant to the part of the construct. We believe that this work holds historical, cultural and/or intellectual importance in the literary works community, therefore despite the oddities, we accounted the work for print as a part of our continuing effort towards preservation of literary work and our contribution towards the development of the society as a whole, driven by our beliefs.

We are grateful to our readers for putting their faith in us and accepting our imperfections with regard to preservation of the historical content. We shall strive hard to meet up to the expectations to improve further to provide an enriching reading experience.

Though, we conduct extensive research in ascertaining the status of copyright before redeveloping a version of the content, in rare cases, a classic work might be incorrectly marked as not-in-copyright. In such cases, if you are the copyright holder, then kindly contact us or write to us, and we shall get back to you with an immediate course of action.

HAPPY READING!

BOHEMIA UNDER HAPSBURG MISRULE

VARIOUS,
THOMAS ČAPEK

ISBN: 978-93-5420-670-2

Published: -

© 2021
LECTOR HOUSE LLP

LECTOR HOUSE LLP
E-MAIL: lectorpublishing@gmail.com

BOHEMIA
UNDER HAPSBURG MISRULE

A STUDY OF THE IDEALS
AND ASPIRATIONS OF THE BOHEMIAN
AND SLOVAK PEOPLES, AS THEY RELATE
TO AND ARE AFFECTED
BY THE GREAT EUROPEAN WAR

EDITED BY

THOMAS ČAPEK

Author of "Slovaks of Hungary," etc.

**DEDICATED
TO THE CAUSE OF
BOHEMIAN-SLOVAK FREEDOM**

*"I trust in God that the
Government of Thine affairs will again revert to Thee, O Bohemian People!"*

JOHN AMOS COMENIUS.

(In exile.)

PREFACE.

The object of this volume is to make Bohemia and her people better known to the English-speaking world. The average Englishman's and American's knowledge of Bohemia is very vague. It is only within recent years that Anglo-American writers have begun to take a deeper interest in her people. Among the more prominent students of Bohemian contemporary life should be mentioned: Will S. Monroe, Emily G. Balch, and Herbert Adolphus Miller, in the United States; and A. R. Colquhoun, Richard J. Kelly, F. P. Marchant, James Baker, Wickham H. Steed, Charles Edmund Maurice, W. R. Morfill, and R. W. Seton-Watson in England. Count Lützow has written in English a number of works on Bohemian matters.

While it is yet too early to foresee the precise results of the Great War, one may judge of coming events by the shadows they cast before them. A close observer of the Austrian shadows is justified in thinking that the Bohemian people, so long suppressed, stand on the threshold of a new destiny. This destiny points to the restoration of their ancient freedom. If the Allies win—and every loyal son of the Land of Hus fervently wishes that their arms might prevail, notwithstanding the fact that Bohemian soldiers are constrained to fight for the cause of the two Kaisers—Bohemia is certain to re-enter the family of self-governing European nations. The proclamation which the Russian Generalissimo addressed to the Poles may be said to apply with equal force to the Bohemians: "The hour has sounded when the sacred dream of your fathers may be realized.... Bohemia will be born again, free in her religion, her language, and autonomous.... The dawn of a new life begins for you.... In this glorious dawn is seen the sign of the cross, the symbol of suffering and the resurrection of a people."

At the close of the Franco-Prussian War, Frenchmen erected in the Place de la Concorde in Paris the Statue of Strassburg, which they have kept draped, as a sign of mourning for the loss of their beloved Alsace-Lorraine. The Bohemians have grieved for their motherland much longer than the French for the "Lost Provinces." Bohemia put on her mourning garb in 1620, the year her rebel army was defeated by the imperialist troops of Ferdinand II., at the Battle of White Mountain near Prague, the capital of the kingdom. May it not be hoped that the joyous moment is near when her sons can substitute for the black and yellow of Austria the red and white of Bohemia—the colors that Charles Havlíček loved so well. "My colors are red and white," declared this fearless patriot to his Austrian tormentors. "You can promise me, you can threaten me, but a traitor I shall never be."

Never during the three hundred years of Austrian misrule were conditions so propitious for throwing off the shackles of oppression as now. In the darkest hours of national humiliation, the children of Hus and of Komenský (Comenius) did not despair. "We existed before Austria," Palacký used to tell them, "and we shall survive her." May not the words of the "Father of his Country," as Palacký was affectionately called by his countrymen, come true, in view of what is taking place in the Hapsburg Monarchy to-day?

With what form of government would Bohemia make her re-entry into the European family of nations—as a free state, as a dependency of Russia, as a ward of the Allies, or incorporated in a federation of the states remaining to the Hapsburg Empire?

It was a favorite theory of Palacký that the Austrian nations would, for their own protection, have to create an Austria, if she were ever destroyed. But what Palacký has said may no longer be true, because the events of 1914 have created issues and opened up possibilities undreamt of in his times. Palacký, let it be understood, had in mind a Confederated Austria that should form a bulwark for small races against German expansion from the north and the west.

It has been intimated that the Allies might agree to create Bohemia and Hungary as independent buffer states to curb German aggression, just as Belgium and Holland are buffer states between Germany and France. If this war has shown anything, it has demonstrated the usefulness of a small state like that of the Belgians. Albania, it will be recalled, had been brought into being by Austria and Italy, not for humanitarian reasons, we may be sure, but to menace and weaken Serbia, of whose growth they were jealous.

Another probability is that Russia might demand, as one of the prizes of war, the cession of the northern part of Austria-Hungary, which is wholly Slavic. She might contend that she could not carry out her traditional policy of guardianship of the Slavs, unless her kinsfolk came under her influence, if not actually under her rule.

Francis Josef waged two wars in the past, both of which ended disastrously for the empire. Yet from both of these wars good has come to his subjects. The campaign in Italy, which resulted in the defeat of the Austrians at Magenta and Solferino in 1859, dealt a severe blow to the bureaucracy, liberating, incidentally, the Italians who were trampled under foot by Radecky. As a result of the war with Prussia in 1866, the Magyars came to their own. Hungarian autonomy dates from 1867. Now it is the turn of the Bohemians to profit from Austria's predicament.

Self-government is not only an ideal but a necessity to Bohemians. Why should Bohemia, in addition to paying for her own needs, make good the deficits of lands which are passive, and in whose domestic affairs she has no greater interest than the State of New York has, for instance, in the local constabulary of Nevada? Year after year Bohemians justly complain that Vienna wrings millions in taxes from them that it spends on lands that are passive. It is partly this feature of the case, the high revenue flowing from the Bohemian Kingdom, which has made Vienna hostile to the home rule agitation. Is it reasonable to suppose, however, that if Austria could not wholly suppress the national aspiration of Bohemians in times of peace, under normal conditions, she is more likely to accomplish it if she returns home from the war exhausted, humiliated, perchance vanquished?

It may seem hazardous to forecast Austria's future in the event of the Allies winning. But this much is already apparent, that the Austria of 1914, the government of which rested on the mediæval idea that one white race was superior to another white race, is doomed to perish. Austria needed a crushing blow from without, such as a lost war, to send toppling the ramshackle structure that has menaced for so long a time the security of the Slavic inhabitants. For, though rent by internal discord, the monarchy obviously lacked forces powerful enough to effect its own redemption. If the Teutonic forces are beaten, the logical sequel will be the breakdown of the Germanic hegemony and a corresponding rise of Slavism. With Poland resuscitated and Serbia strengthened, Vienna, it is certain, will be powerless to hold the Bohemians down.

But no matter what may happen, whether Austria-Hungary will remain Hapsburg, whether the Allies will impose their will on her destiny, or whether the Russians will become the masters of the North Slavs, let us hope that the future map-makers will not be military conquerors, as was the case at the Congress of Vienna in 1814, or statesmen of the Bismarck type, who, at the Berlin Congress in 1878, were determined to separate the people of one race, instead of uniting them. Let the map-makers be ethnologists who will, wherever practicable, deliminate boundaries according to racial, not political lines, giving German territory to the Germans, Magyar territory to the people of that race, Slavic lands to the Slavs.

Bohemia would not assume the serious task of self-government as an inexperienced novice. Bohemia is one of the oldest states in Central Europe. As a kingdom she antedates the German kingdoms, not excepting Prussia, Saxony, Bavaria. Some of these were yet minor states when she already played a conspicuous rôle in the affairs of Europe. In point of population the United States of Bohemia — including Bohemia herself, Moravia, Silesia, and Slovakland — would have within her borders a population numbering about 12,000,000. The combined area of the three first-named states is almost twice the size of Switzerland. Prague, the capital, had in 1910 581,163 inhabitants. As a wealth-providing and revenue-yielding country Bohemia stands unrivalled among the Hapsburg States.

T. Č.

New York

CONTENTS

I.

HAVE THE BOHEMIANS A PLACE IN THE SUN?

Bohemia (German Böhmen, Bohemian Čechy[1]) has an area of 20,223 square miles, and is bounded on the north by Saxony and Prussian Silesia; on the east by Prussia and Moravia; on the south by Lower Austria; on the west by Bavaria. According to the census of 1910, 4,241,918 inhabitants declared for Bohemian and 2,467,724 for the German language.

Historians recognize two epochal events in the life of the nation. The first begins with the outbreak of the Hussite wars, following the death of King Václav IV. in 1419; the second, with the battle of White Mountain in 1620. The period intervening between the first two events is referred to as the Middle Age. That which preceded the Hussite wars is called the Old Age, and, that which followed the defeat at White Mountain, the New Age.

THE LAND AND THE PEOPLE.

The Margravate of Moravia, a sister state of Bohemia, and one of her crown-lands, contains an area of 8,583 square miles. The population of Moravia is 1,868,971 Bohemians and 719,435 Germans.

The third crown-land of Bohemia is the Duchy of Silesia, with an area of 1,987 square miles. The population is divided as follows: 180,348 Bohemians, 325,523 Germans, 235,224 Poles.[2]

[1] The word Czech, which is being freely used in the Anglo-American press, is a corrupt form of Čech. The German form is Czech, Tscheche, the French Tchèque. But, inasmuch as Čech is sounded more nearly like Checkh and not Czech, the form Czech fails utterly of its purpose and its use should be discontinued. The people themselves prefer to be called Bohemians, not Czechs, which latter appellation is not generally known or understood. Some years ago a noted scholar was severely censured because he named his magazine, edited in the German language, but Bohemiophile in tendency, "Čechische Revue," instead of "Böhmische Revue." The truth of the matter is that the appellation Czech is an invention of Vienna journalists, who, by persistent use of the term, wish to give a warning to the world that Bohemia is not all Čech, but part German and part Čech.

[2] Silesia was much larger, but Frederick II. of Prussia despoiled Maria Theresa in 1742 of a major portion of it. Thus was created Prussian Silesia and Austrian Silesia. In Macaulay's "Life of Frederick the Great," we read why the Prussian King made war on his neighbor. In manifestoes he might, for form's sake, insert some idle stories about his antiquated claim on Silesia; but in his conversations and Memoirs he took a very different tone. His own words were: "Ambition, interest, the desire of making people talk about me, carried the day; and I decided for war." If there is a rectification of Prussian boundary after

Although statisticians found in Austria, in 1910, only 6,435,983 Bohemians, it is generally known that the actual figure is higher by several hundred thousands. Singularly enough, the test in Austria of one's nationality is not the mother tongue of the citizen, as elsewhere, but the lingual medium which one employs in daily association with others. This medium the statisticians designate the "Verkehrsprache"—the "Language of Association." The first decennial census, under this novel system, was taken in 1880, and the results thereby obtained pleased Vienna so well that the method has remained in use ever since. When the matter was debated in parliament in 1880 the Bohemians and other Slavs indignantly protested against it as unscientific and as a device dictated by political motives. A census so taken, they contended, was calculated to raise by artful means the numerical strength of the Germans and to deduce from it the superior importance to the state of the Germanic element to the disadvantage of the non-Germans.[3] It was argued that the mother tongue of the citizens should serve as the test of one's nationality, not the language in which the Slavic workman may be compelled to address his German employer or a Slavic subaltern his German military superior. But, as usual, Slavic opposition was over-ridden. Even fair-minded Austrians condemned the system as unscientific. Innama-Sternegg, for instance, deplored the fact that the empire should have recourse to the "Verkehrsprache" test for political purposes. On this ground Austrian official figures should be scrutinized with extreme caution. It has repeatedly been proven by private census-takers that the official census is unreliable, and that it grossly underestimates the numerical strength of the Bohemians.

From an agricultural state, that it was until recently, Bohemia is rapidly changing into an industrial state. Two of the most valuable products, which make for the wealth of industrial countries, namely, coal and iron, the hills of Bohemia contain in abundance. Among her specialties, which have acquired world-wide renown, are decorated and engraved glassware, beer (Pilsener), high-class cotton textiles and linen goods, grass seeds, embroidery, hops, fezzes worn by the Mohammedan people of the Orient, toys, etc.

From times immemorial, Bohemia has been the battle-ground between the Slav and the Teuton. A glance at the map of Central Europe will tell the story. Most westerly of all the Slavic peoples, the Bohemians are surrounded on the north, west, and south by Germans. Only on the south and east frontiers are there strips of territory that connect them with kindred races. More than once the Germanic sea has threatened to engulf them in the same way that it swept away the Slavic tribes that lived north of them in Lusatia and of whose existence nothing now remains but the Slavic names of rivers and cities. The struggle for supremacy in Bohemia may be said to have begun the year the fabled leader Čech, in the gray

---

the war, a portion of Prussian Silesia, that is still Bohemian, should be returned to Austrian Silesia.

[3] Representation in parliament being determinable by the result of the enumeration, one can at once see of what vital concern it is to non-Germans to obtain a census free from political bias. As matters are, the Germans constitute 35 per cent. of the population, yet have 52 per cent. representation in the Reichsrath (parliament), while 24 per cent. Bohemians are represented in parliament only by 17 per cent.

dawn of history (about 450 A.D.), migrated to the country, having dispossessed the non-Slavic tribes of Boii, from whom Bohemia acquired her name. The Hussite wars in the fifteenth century are popularly believed to have been waged to free men's intellects from the spiritual trammels of Rome; yet in the last analysis it will be found that the Hussites, in making war on the invaders who poured into the country from Germany, rejoiced in vanquishing alike the foes of their race and the oppressors of their conscience. Such, at least, is the conviction that one acquires in perusing those chapters of the history of the country that treat of the Hussite wars.

Jointly with Moravia, Bohemia formed the nucleus of the Bohemian State; this state had never ceased to be Bohemian-Slavic in character, though at times ruled by alien kings. The whole of Silesia and both Lusatias (Upper and Lower) also constituted part and parcel of this state, yet the latter were never so closely affiliated with Bohemia as Moravia had been, because the inhabitants of the Lusatias were not by origin or preponderatingly Bohemian, but of Polish and Serb (Wend) ancestry, having been largely Germanized at the time they passed under the rule of the Bohemian Kings in the fourteenth century.

Generally speaking, the Bohemians inhabited the flat lands of the interior, while the Germans overflowed the border line on the south, west, and north, forming an almost uninterrupted chain of settlements. As a matter of fact, however, there is no compact, unmixed German territory in Bohemia, which is exclusively German and into which the Bohemian workman, going in search of employment to the mines, mills, and shops in the northwest, has not penetrated, and in which he has not domiciled himself. The invasion of Bohemian workmen has virtually rendered bilingual every such Germanized district where industrialism flourishes.

So intermixed are the two races on the border line that a person cannot say confidently that his ancestry is either pure German or pure Bohemian. Observe, for example, the names of Bohemian leaders: Rieger, Brauner, Grégr, Zeithammer. They have an unmistakable Teutonic ring. Again, note the names of Schmeykal, Tascheck, Chlumecky, and Giskra, who lead the German cohorts. These clearly betray Slavic origin. It has been remarked sarcastically that the Bohemians were really German-speaking Slavs. Certain it is that their association of more than a thousand years' duration with Teutonic neighbors resulted in their accepting many of the latter's customs and western culture. Then, too, foreigners have noticed in Bohemians a degree of aggressiveness that they claim is singularly lacking in the make-up of the other Slavs. This trait, aggressiveness, may have been inherited as a result of an almost ceaseless struggle for national existence. It is not improbable, however, that the racial mixture above mentioned may have been one of the contributing causes.

Fear of the Teutonic peril has always harried the soul of the nation. Every historian, every poet, every patriot has admonished the people to be on their guard. One of the oldest chorals extant contains the pathetic invocation to the patron saint of the country. "St. Václav, Duke of the Bohemian Land, do not let us perish nor our descendants."

In course of time many Germans and denationalized Bohemians were Bohemianized, so that it is hazardous to guess whether in Bohemia and Moravia more Germans adopted the Bohemian language than Bohemians the German. The final sum of this process of assimilation seems to be that the Bohemians constitute more than two-thirds and the Germans less than one-third of the entire population of the kingdom.

As regards the ownership of land, Bohemians hold about three-fifths of the soil, in Moravia three-fourths. If it is true that the people with a future is the one that owns the land, then the future of Bohemians is clearly assured. Looking backward, it was very fortunate for the nation that in the days of its deepest abasement the peasant was not allowed to dispose of his holdings at will, otherwise the inrush of the Teutons would have still more reduced the national area.

If we accept literacy as one of the tests of the culture of a people, it will be found that the Bohemians rank highest among the Slavic races, surpassing even Austrian-Germans and Hungarian Magyars. According to the official reports of the Commissioner of Immigration in Washington, the number of illiterates among Bohemians is less than 3 per cent., Slovaks 25 per cent., Serbo-Croatians, 38 per cent., Poles 40 per cent., Little Russians (Ruthenes), 63 per cent. Among the non-Slavic immigrants from Austria-Hungary to America the percentages of illiteracy are as follows: Germans 4 per cent., Magyars 12 per cent., Italians 23 per cent., Jews 23 per cent., Rumuns 29 per cent.

It may not be uninteresting to note, as indicative of the position held by Bohemians among the Slavs, the number of newspapers circulated in Slavdom.[4] The Lusatian Serbs, a remnant of a once populous Slavic branch in Germany, support 11 publications; Slovaks, 53 (4 of which are dailies); Slovenes, 110 (5 dailies); Bulgars, 300 (19 dailies); Serbo-Croatians, 350 (37 dailies); Poles, 600 (78 dailies); Bohemians, 1,400 (34 dailies), and Russians, 1,800 (315 dailies). From this statistical fragment it will be seen that a little country like Bohemia takes very favorable rank when compared with the great Russian Empire.

At home the Bohemian is looked upon as a progressive agriculturist, and American tourists who have traveled in the country have been favorably impressed with the orderliness of the farms and the high state of cultivation of the land. In the great agricultural belt formed by the States of Wisconsin, Minnesota, Iowa, Nebraska, Kansas, and the Dakotas there are large settlements of Bohemians (about one-half of the Bohemian population in the United States devoting itself to farming), and their farms are known to bear favorable comparison with the homesteads owned by land-tillers of Scandinavian and Teuton ancestry.

The fact that a particular faith was denied him and he was required to accept a different creed, has made the Bohemian one of the most liberal-minded of men,—in many instances a sceptic and a scoffer. Possibly there is no other foreign nationality in the United States that can boast translations in the vernacular of Thomas Paine and of other advanced thinkers as early as the Bohemians.

Economically the Germans are stronger than any other one race in the empire. Much of their unquestioned primacy in the realm of commerce and industry is

[4] "The Slavdom: Picture of Its Past and Present," Prague, 1912.

due to the fact that everywhere they enjoy special favors from the government. Then, too, the Slav, who is by preference a land-tiller (as is also the Magyar), is still a novice in business. The vast economic interests of the Jews are found wholly on the side of the Germans. Ernest Denis believes that German primacy in commerce may yet continue for some time to come, because the districts inhabited by them in Bohemia offer greater inducements to the investor and the capitalist, owing to the wealth of mineral riches found along the northwest frontier. It is, however, Denis' opinion that the existing inequality in the distribution of industrial wealth will diminish as years go by; democracy, marching as it does everywhere at the expense of the upper classes, will level it down and give the Bohemian majority its share in commerce and industry.

THE DOWNFALL.

The Bohemians preserved their independence till 1620. That year they rebelled against the king for political and religious reasons and were defeated at the battle of White Hill (Bílá Hora) near Prague. From the effects of this disastrous event the nation has never recovered, for even now, after the lapse of 295 years, the scars received at Bílá Hora are not wholly healed.

Ferdinand II. punished the rebels with traditional Austrian fury. On June 21, 1621, he caused the execution at Prague of twenty-seven leaders of the revolution—all men belonging to the most noted families in the country. A number of them were condemned to humiliating physical punishment and the estates of all were confiscated. The first to lay his head on the block of the executioner was Count Joachim Andrew Šlik (Schlick). During the interregnum Šlik had been a Director; besides, he had served as Chief Justice and Governor of Upper Lusatia. The next victim was Václav Budovec of Budova, "a man of splendid talents and illustrious learning, distinguished as a writer, widely known as a traveler, and an ornament to his country." Pelcl said of Budova that he belonged "to that old cast of serious, thoughtful, inflexible Bohemians, by which the nation was characterized in the fifteenth and sixteenth centuries." The third to suffer was Christopher Harant of Polžic, "a learned man, distinguished writer, and noted traveler." The next on the death list was Caspar Kaplíř of Sulevic, a venerable man of eighty-six. The fifth was Prokop Dvořecký of Olbramovic, a scion of an old family. The sixth was Baron Frederick Bílý, "an upright and learned man, one of the Directors at the time of the interregnum." The seventh, Henry Otto of Los, who, under Frederick, was connected with the exchequer. Then followed successively Dionys Černín, William Konechlumský, aged seventy years, Bohuslav of Michalovic, "a man of splendid talents who deserved well of his country," Valentine Kochan of Prachov, a learned master of arts; Tobias Štefek of Koloděj, a citizen of Prague and a Director of the Revolution; John Jesenský of Jesen (Jessenius), a scholar, scientist, and orator, "whose writings shed lustre on the university;" Christopher Kober, a noted citizen of Prague; Burgomasters John Šultys of Kutná Hora and Maximilian Hošťálek of Žatec (Saaz), (the two latter having been Directors during the interregnum), John Kutnaur, a Councilor of Prague, Kutnaur's father-in-law Simon Sušický, Nathaniel Vodňanský of Uračov, Václav Jizbický. The last to undergo death were Henry

Kozel, Andrew Kocour of Otín, George Řecický, Michael Wittman, Simon Vokáč of Chyš and Špicberk, Leander Rüppel, and George Hauenschild. On the tower of the ancient Charles Bridge, which connects the Old Town with the Small Town in Prague, twelve heads of the rebels were set up in small wire cages, six on each side of the tower, to awe the populace. There these gruesome evidences of Hapsburg hatred remained for years. On the same tower were exposed to public view the hands of Šlik and Michalovic and the tongue of Jesenský. Rüppel's head and hand were nailed on the wall of the Town House.

So ended the "Bloody Day at Prague"—a day that Bohemians may have forgiven, but which none have forgotten. What now followed is probably without parallel in the history of European nations. Edmund de Schweinitz, in commenting on the consequences of the Bohemian Revolution, says that "in the history of Christendom there were few events more mournful. From the pinnacle of prosperity Bohemia and Moravia were plunged into the depths of adversity."

The month the executions took place, the emperor, or rather the so-called Liechtenstein's Commission on Confiscations which had been appointed by the emperor, pronounced forfeiture on the estates of 658 landowners of the nobility out of a total of 728, whose names were on the list of accused. Thomas Bílek, a writer of unimpeachable authority, has published a voluminous book on these confiscations from which it would appear that the Liechtenstein Commission had confiscated fully two-thirds of all the lands in Bohemia. Some of the choicest estates taken away from the rebels the emperor retained for the Hapsburg family. A goodly portion of the forfeited lands was given to the church, of which the emperor was a devout member. "Take, fathers, take," he used to say to the ecclesiastics when endowing this or that foundation with gifts of confiscated estates. "It is not always that you will have a Ferdinand." Still other lands reverted to the state. What was left the emperor magnanimously distributed among those of his favorites whose military prowess in the rebellion entitled them to some special recognition or compensation. Albrecht, Count of Wallenstein or Waldstein, at one time a Generalissimo of Ferdinand's army against Gustavus Adolphus, was able to "purchase" sixty confiscated estates of an enormous value.

Struve has remarked that of all the nobles in the world those in the Hapsburg Monarchy had probably the least reason to boast of their ancestry. This is especially true of the nobility whose advent into Bohemia antedates the first half of the seventeenth century. From the events here related began the rise in Bohemia of such families as Buquoy, Clary de Riva, Aldringen, Trautmansdorff, Metternich, Marradas, Verduga, Colloredo, Piccolomini, Wallis, Gallas, Millesimo, Liechtenstein, Goltz, Villani, Defours, Huerta, Vasques—names indicating Spanish, Italian, German, and Walloon birth. These aliens, enriched by property taken away from Bohemian nobility, surrounded themselves with foreign officials, who treated the natives with the scorn and insolence of victors. Their châteaux formed in many cases the nucleus of German settlements which later threatened to overwhelm the nation. Some of these "islands," or settlements, which were situated farther inland, were in time absorbed by the native population. But not so with the colonies on the border. These latter not only preserved the lingual and national characteristics of the owners, but they even contrived to Germanize the home element that came into contact with them. It was during this calamitous period that the Germans made the greatest inroads upon Bohemian national territory.

Prior to the Thirty Years' War Bohemia was overwhelmingly Protestant,[5] but Ferdinand determined that in his empire there should be "unity of faith and tongue." A unity of faith he and his successors have achieved, but it has been denied to the Hapsburgs—much as they have tried to achieve it—the unity of language.

In 1620 Jesuit fathers were invited to come to Bohemia and to take charge of the once renowned University of Prague and of the provincial schools. "The Jesuits buried the spirit of the Bohemian nation for centuries." This is the severe judgment of no less a person than V. V. Tomek, the noted historian. Accompanied by Liechtenstein's dragoons these ecclesiastics went from town to town, searched libraries, carried off books written in Bohemian and burned them whether they were "tainted" or not. Sometimes the books were privately thrown in the flames in the houses where they had been seized; at other times they were brought to the market-place or to the public gallows and there publicly burned. The Jesuits were indefatigable in their search for heretical literature, ransacking houses from cellar to garret, opening every closet and chest, prying into the very dog kennels and pig-sties. People hid their most precious books from the ferreting eyes of the inquisitioners in baking ovens, cellars, and caves. There are cases on record of rare Bohemian volumes having been saved from destruction by being hidden under manure piles.

One zealot, Koniáš by name, boasted that he had burned or otherwise mutilated 60,000 Bohemian volumes. According to him "all Bohemian books printed between the years 1414 and 1620, treating of religious subjects, were generally dangerous and suspicious." From their seat in the Clementinum (Prague University) they presided over the intellectual life of the country; that is to say, they wholly suppressed it. In order to more systematically supervise the work, a censor was appointed by them for each of the three lands,—Bohemia, Moravia, and Silesia,—and it was the duty of this censor to see to it that no books were published or reprinted that did not meet the approval of the general of the order. Easy was the labor of the censor, for in Moravia, for instance, only one printer was fortunate enough to secure a license. In Bohemia they set up the so-called University Printing Office. Besides this only five or six other establishments were licensed to print books. In a few decades these zealots destroyed Bohemian literature altogether. The almanacs, tracts, hymnals, and prayer books that issued from their printing presses could not be dignified by the term literature. Count Lützow, in his "History of Bohemian Literature," frankly admits that, with few exceptions, all the men who, during the last years of Bohemian independence, were most prominent in literature and politics belonged to the Bohemian Church. Living in exile in foreign

---

[5] Now of every 1,000 inhabitants in Bohemia 956.61 profess the Catholic faith. Due to various reasons—spiritual, political, and historical—more than one-half of the American Bohemians have seceded from the Catholic Church. Some have joined various Protestant sects, but the majority of the secessionists are Free-thinkers.

countries, there was no one left at home to resume their tasks.

Ferdinand began his anti-reformation crusade in earnest in 1621. In December of that year he issued a patent by virtue of which about one thousand teachers and ministers of the gospel of the Bohemian Church were forced to leave the country. The Lutherans did not come under this ban, inasmuch as the emperor was anxious to please his ally, the Elector of Saxony, who pleaded clemency for his co-religionists. In 1624 seven patents were promulgated. Some of these were directed against the laity, which, till then, had escaped the wrath of the conqueror. It ordered the expulsion from trade guilds of all those who could not agree with the emperor in matters of faith. Discriminatory measures against nonconformist merchants and traders went into effect, which quickly resulted in their ruin. Another patent, bearing date July 31, 1627, was more severe than those preceding it. By it dissenters of both sexes and irrespective of rank were ordered to renounce their faith within six months, or failing to do so, leave the country. The operation of this patent extended to Moravia, but not to Silesia and Lusatia. The two latter-named provinces had been spared because of a promise given by the emperor to the Elector of Saxony.

So severely did the country suffer by forced expatriation, as a result of these edicts, that Ferdinand saw himself compelled to issue other patents to check it. In the hope of conciliating he remitted fines in certain cases, discontinued suits for treason, and made restitution of confiscated property. In some cases he extended the time within which heretics could become reconciled with the church, but the clemency was extended too late, for while some individuals yielded to the formidable pressure, the great mass of nonconformists, comprising the very flower of the nation, were determined rather to lose their property and leave the fatherland than to renounce that which they held most sacred.

Count Slavata, who himself took no inconsiderable part in this terrible drama of anti-reformation, and who, owing to his religious convictions, cannot be accused of partiality, is authority for the statement that about 36,000 families, including 185 houses of nobility (some of these houses numbered as many as 50 persons each), statesmen, distinguished authors, professors, preachers,—spurning to accept the emperor's terms, went into exile.

In 1627 Ferdinand promulgated what he designated the "Amended Statute." The "amendment" really consisted in the abolishment of those ancient rights and liberties of the land which were incompatible with autocratic powers.

Under the "Amended Statute" the kingdom, heretofore free to elect its sovereign, was declared to be an hereditary possession, both in the male and female line, of the Hapsburg family. The three estates—lords, knights, and the cities—which till then constituted the legislative branch of the government, were augmented by a fourth unit, the clergy. The fourth estate was destined to exercise, as subsequent events have shown, the greatest influence on the affairs of the government. The Diet at Prague was divested practically of all its power and initiative; from now on its sole function was to levy and collect taxes. And because the king had invited to the country so many alien nobles (or commoners later ennobled) who were ignorant of the language of the land, the amended statute provided that henceforth the German language should enjoy equal rights with the Bohemian. A disastrous blow to the unity of the Bohemian Crown was further dealt by the annulment of the right of the estates in Bohemia, Moravia, and Silesia to meet at a General Assembly for the purpose of deliberating on matters common to the crown. By this clever stroke the emperor tore asunder the ancient ties of the kingdom. He rightly reasoned that by isolating each of the integral parts of the kingdom he could easier hope to hold in leash the whole of it.

In time the administration of the Bohemian Crown was entrusted to an executive who received the title of Chancellor, and when the kings no longer resided in Prague, having taken up a permanent abode in Vienna, the Chancellory was removed thither, ostensibly on the ground that the Chancellor was required to be near the person of the sovereign. In reality, however, the transfer was a part of a preconceived plan to make Vienna the centre of the empire, from which the Hapsburg "provinces" were to be ruled. Under one pretext or another the Chancellory was being gradually shorn of its powers, until Maria Theresa (1740-1780) abolished it altogether. Henceforth even purely local matters were administered from Vienna direct, and the officials began to style the once proud kingdom a "province of Austria."

During the Thirty Years' War thousands of villages were destroyed by fire and many of them have never been rebuilt. The population, which before the war was estimated at 3,000,000, was reduced by fire, sword, and pestilence to about 800,000. Fields lay fallow for years for lack of workers to cultivate them. Of the 151,000 farms before the war hardly 50,000 remained. Native nobility was reduced to beggary by the confiscation of their estates, and the peasantry that survived was reduced by alien lords to a degrading condition of serfdom. Between 1621 and 1630 400 Prague citizens went into exile. The Nové Město (one of the Prague quarters) alone had at one time 500 vacant houses. The town of Žatec, which in 1618 had 460 citizens, counted ten years later 205 of them. In Kutná Hora, of a total of 600 houses, 200 remained without owners or tenants. The population of the city of Olomouc in Moravia, by 1640, was reduced from 30,000 to 1,670. Wherever the armies marched nothing was seen but waste and ruins. According to notes taken by Swedish soldiers, 138 cities and 2,171 villages were totally ravaged by fire. The textile industry, which had been the source of the wealth of the country, was almost wholly destroyed by the war.

The defeat at White Mountain could not have been productive of such disastrous consequences had it not been for the fact that the nobles were the standard-bearers of Bohemian nationalism and the sole representatives of the nation's culture and traditions. The peasantry in those days and for a long time afterward was yet helplessly dependent on the aristocracy.

Bohemian Huguenots were scattered over every land in Central Europe, most of them seeking refuge in nearby Saxony, Silesia, Hungary, and Poland. Many emigrated to more distant lands, such as Sweden, serving in the army of Gustavus Adolphus, Russia, Holland, England. A few of the more adventurous spirits wandered off with the English and the Dutch to America. One of them, Augustine Herman, a noted figure among the early Dutch in New Amsterdam, made an attempt to establish a colony of compatriots on a grant of land that he had received from Lord Baltimore and which he named in honor of his native land, Bohemia Manor, a place famous in early Maryland history. Numerous exiles settled in the first half of the seventeenth century in Virginia. In the beginning the exiles hoped to be permitted to return home, but the terms of the Peace of Westphalia (1648) made such a return definitely impossible. They repeatedly called for help. Oliver Cromwell, it is said, had a project under consideration whereby Bohemian exiles were to be settled in Ireland. John Amos Comenius, the bishop of the Bohemian Church, a distinguished educator, himself an exile living in Holland, presented the history of his church to King Charles II. of England in 1660, with a stirring account of its suffering.

Suspecting that the dissenters were yet unsuppressed, the government caused other patents to be issued, one of which, published in 1650, imposed severe penalties such as the billeting of troops, banishment from the country, confiscation of property and, in extreme cases, death. A patent dated April 9th of that year required that within six weeks all parishes should instal conformist clergy or close. Under Josef I. (1705-1711), and again under Charles VI. (1711-1740), the work of anti-reformation was renewed with increased severity. Loyal subjects were enjoined under pain of death from harboring or aiding heretic teachers or ministers, the reading and smuggling into the country or otherwise circulating Bohemian books on the prohibited list. Other patents followed in 1721, 1722, 1723, 1724, 1725, 1726, with the result that non-Catholics who still secretly clung to the forbidden faith emigrated to Saxony and Prussia, where they sought the protection of the rulers of those countries. The suffering of the unfortunates was somewhat, though not wholly, relieved when the German princes, assembled in the Diet at Regensburg in 1735, sent a strong appeal to the Austrian Emperor to treat his subjects with more toleration. When the Edict of Toleration was issued in 1781, permitting free worship, there still remained in Bohemia about 100,000 Protestants.[6] Of the refugees who fled to Germany in the first quarter of the eighteenth century many found their way with the Herrnhuters, or Moravians, as they are called in the United States, to Georgia, and others to Pennsylvania, where they established, in 1741, the flourishing town of Bethlehem, now the recognized centre of the Moravian Church in the United States.[7]

---

[6] However, the Patent of Tolerance extended only to Protestants of the Helvetian and Augsburg Confessions, not to the Bohemian Church, which latter had been denied recognition.

[7] On February 9, 1748, a bill was introduced in the English Parliament "to relieve the United Brethren (so-called in Comenius' time), or Moravians, from military duties and taking oaths." Among the speakers was General Oglethorpe, who spoke in support of the bill. "In the year 1683 a most pathetic account of these brethren was published by order of Archbishop Sancroft and Bishop Compton," said Oglethorpe. "They also addressed the Church of England in the year 1715, being reduced to a very low ebb in Poland, and his late Majesty, George I., by the recommendation of the late Archbishop Wake, gave orders in council for the relief of these Reformed Episcopal Churches, and letters patent for their support were issued soon after. But since 1724 circumstances have altered for the better, and they have wonderfully revived, increased and spread in several countries. They have even made some settlements in America. In the province of Pennsylvania they have about 800

GERMANIZATION AND THE AWAKENING.

Germanization, as a matter of fact, was pursued in Bohemia by every Hapsburg, though the rulers of that house have not planned it as systematically as Maria Theresa or her son, Josef II. Centralism, to be successful and powerful, required the levelling of the differences of speech and of race. Every Hapsburg ruler had been educated to the belief that he was rendering a supreme service to his subjects by forcing them "to unlearn the barbaric language of their sires, which isolated them from the rest of the world." "He who knows only Bohemian and Latin," declared Councilor Gebler, in 1765, "is bound to make a poor scholar, and it were better for him to stick to the plow and to the trade; there are too many Latin scholars as it is." More and more the conviction gained ground that a language like the Bohemian, spoken but by a few millions of people, was valueless, and that it would be a folly for the government to aid in its restoration.

Austrian statesmen were determined to impose German at one time even on the unsuspecting Galicians, though in Galicia there were no Germans at all, only Poles and Russians. Discoursing upon the worth or the lack of value of languages of small nations, Denis says: "These arguments may be true, but unfortunately they could be applied to every language in the world."

In 1774 a detailed plan for the Germanization of schools in the empire was submitted to Maria Theresa. This plan provided for German schools and none others. By "mother" language was meant the German. Bohemian was permitted in the primary or lowest grades of the school. No pupil could enter a gymnasium (secondary school) who had not had a previous training in German. Fortunately for the non-Germans of that period, progress was less rapid than had been generally expected. Schoolmasters were scarce and pupils, not understanding the language of the teachers, advanced but slowly. As a result of all this, the queen, though unwilling, was compelled to make concessions here and there and to proceed less aggressively.

A noted writer has truthfully said that in the eighteenth century Bohemians were outcasts in their own country. A lad who wanted to learn a trade had to attend a German school for apprentices, and only pupils knowing German were entitled to receive stipends. In the secondary schools in Bohemia the vernacular was treated as a "foreign" language. A professor was required to qualify in Latin and Greek, yet no one questioned whether or not he knew the tongue of the natives. Pupils were educated in German to be able to perform the work of janissaries on the people of their own race. Slowly but steadily Bohemian was likewise forced out of the courts. Laws were promulgated in the German language. The Bohemian began to lose ground in the highest courts of justice; gradually it was forced out from the inferior courts. After 1749 law documents in Bohemian became rarer. When, in 1788, Count Cavriani moved that only certain notices be published in that language, the motion was passed without opposition. From that time on German took its place as the official language in the kingdom.

Can we wonder then that, pressed as it was on four sides—by the church, the

people to whom the proprietor and Governor gave very good character."

state, the school, and the dominant classes of the population—the tongue of Hus and Comenius lost ground almost altogether? And who saved it from utter extinction? It was the lowly peasant who continued giving it shelter under his thatched roof, long after it had been expelled from the proud châteaux of the nobility and disowned by the middle classes. The peasant preserved the language for the literary men who rescued from oblivion this precious gift for future generations. "It is admitted by all," said Palacký, "that the resuscitation of the nation was accomplished wholly by our writers. These men saved the language; they carried the banner which they wished the nation to follow. Literature was the fountain spring of our national life, and the literati placed themselves at the forefront of the revivalist movement."

The diet of the kingdom recommended, in 1790, that Bohemian should be introduced at least in certain secondary schools, preferably in Prague, but the Austrian world of officialdom was opposed even to this concession. "No one threatens the life of the Bohemian tongue," protested these officials. "The government cannot antagonize the feeling of the most influential and wealthiest classes who use German, if not exclusively, at least overwhelmingly. Moreover, to encourage Bohemian would be to lose sight of the idea of the unification of the empire. The state must not deprive the Bohemians of the blessing and of the opportunity that emanate from the knowledge of German. Useful though Bohemian may be, its study must not be at the expense of German."

Two important events, both of which occurred toward the end of the eighteenth century, helped to awaken the soul of the prostrate nation. One was the determination of Emperor Josef II. to make the empire a German state, as has already been pointed out. But a greater incentive than Josef's coercive measures were the inspiring ideals of the first French Revolution which found their way even to far-off Bohemia. The motto of the French revolutionists, "Liberty, equality, fraternity," could not fail to give hope to the handful of Bohemian intellectuals.[8]

However, as late as 1848, the year of revolutionary changes in Austria, the Bohemian language was still a Cinderella in its own land. In the streets of Prague it was rarely spoken by the people of any social distinction. To engage in Bohemian conversation with strangers was a risky undertaking, unless one was prepared to be rebuked in the sternest manner. German predominated, except in stores that were patronized by apprentices and peddlers. Posters solely in Bohemian were not allowed by the police. The text had to be translated, and the German part of it

---

[8] When Napoleon sought to weaken Austria's position at home, he addressed a patriotic appeal to the Bohemians. "Your union with Austria," read Napoleon's appeal, "has been your misfortune. Your blood has been shed for her in distant lands, and your dearest interests have been sacrificed continually to those of the hereditary provinces. You form the finest portion of her empire, and you are treated as a mere province to be used as an instrument of passions to which you are strangers. You have national customs and a national language; you pride yourself on your ancient and illustrious origin. Assume once more your position as a nation. Choose a king for yourselves, who shall reign for you alone, who shall dwell in your midst and be surrounded by your citizens and your soldiers."—Napoleon's proclamation found no echo among the people for whom it was intended. The sentiment of nationality was yet too weak to respond.

printed above the Bohemian. Nowhere but in the households of the commonest classes was the despised tongue sheltered. Families belonging to the world of officialdom and to the wealthier bourgeoisie, though often imperfectly familiar with it, clung to German. Strict etiquette barred Bohemian from the salons. The only entrance that was open to it led through the halls of the servants. So completely were the people denationalized that foreigners visiting the resorts at Carlsbad and Marienbad expressed their astonishment on hearing the peasants talk in an unknown tongue. They had learned to look upon Bohemia as a part of Germany and on the inhabitants as Germans. Particularly the Russians and the Poles were surprised to meet kinsmen in Bohemia whose language sounded familiar to their ears.

"A few of us," writes Jacob Malý, one of the staunch patriots of that time, "met each Thursday at the Black Horse (a first-class hotel in Prague) and gave orders to the waiters in Bohemian, who, of course, understood us well. This we did with the intention of giving encouragement to others; but seeing the futility of our efforts in this direction, we gave up the propaganda in disgust."

In 1852, the then chief of police of Prague confidently predicted that in fifty years there would be no Bohemians in Prague. That even Austrian Chiefs of Police could make a mistake, appears from the fact that Greater Prague to-day numbers nearly 600,000 inhabitants, of whom only about 17,000 are Germans. When, in 1844, Archduke Stephen came to Prague and the citizens arranged a torch procession in his honor, the police were scandalized to hear, mingling with the customary "Vivat," shouts in Bohemian, "Sláva!"

Authors and newspaper writers were objects of unbounded curiosity. Malý, already quoted, relates the following: "Walking in the streets of Prague, I often noticed people pointing at me and saying: 'Das ist auch einer von den Vlastenzen' (Here goes another of those patriots), or 'Das ist ein gewaltiger Czeche' (There is a thorough Čech for you). During my stay in southern Bohemia in 1838, the innkeeper of a tavern which I frequented evenings had surely no reason to regret my patronage, for people would come primarily to have a peep at me."

In the biography of Palacký[9] we read an account of a memorable meeting of patriots held in 1825 in the Sternberg Palace in Prague. Palacký being invited to dinner on that particular day, as he often had been, remained in the company of the Counts Sternberg until midnight. A violent dispute that arose between the

---

[9] Francis Palacký (1798-1876), historian, revivalist, and statesman, is, by common consent, regarded as the greatest Bohemian of our time. His monumental work, "History of the Bohemian Nation," on which he labored some thirty years, will endure as long as the Bohemian language continues to be spoken. There was a time when not only the outside world, but Bohemians themselves, believed that the old-time Bohemians of the stormy days of John Hus or those who revolted against Ferdinand II. were a band of heretics and rebels. Such has been the official Austrian version of these events in Bohemia. However, the truth could not be suppressed for all time. Palacký and others were being born, and in time the alluvium of Austrian bigotry and of falsehood was removed from the nation's past, and to the astonished gaze of Resurrected Bohemia was revealed a glorious history of which descendants could be justly proud. Great men, national heroes, hitherto unknown or misunderstood, emerged from almost every chapter of Palacký's work.

guests and the hosts would not allow of their separation. Among other questions discussed was the prospective publication of a scientific magazine in both languages, Bohemian and German. Abbé Dobrovský, the "father of Slavic philology," and Count Kaspar were of the opinion that it was too late to think seriously of the resuscitation of the Bohemian nation, and that all attempts in that direction must end in failure. Palacký, then a youthful enthusiast, disagreed in this with his elder companions and bitterly reproached Dobrovský, that he, a literary light among his people, had not written a single book in the mother tongue. "Were we all to do the same, then indeed our nation would perish for lack of intellectual nourishment. As for me," fervently argued Palacký, "were I but a gypsy by birth, and the last of that race, I would still deem it my duty to try to perpetuate an honorable mention of it in the annals of mankind." Count Sternberg, though he knew the language well, never used it in conversation with people of education. He availed himself of it only when talking with his servants.

In 1811 Dobrovský wrote to the noted Slovene scholar, Kopitar, that "the cause of the nation is desperate, unless God helps." In his discourse, "Geschichte der Deutschen und ihrer Sprache in Böhmen," dated 1790, Pelcl expressed himself as follows: "The time is approaching when the Bohemian language will be in the same situation at home as the Slavonic language is to-day in Miess, Brandenburg, and Silesia, where German is everywhere prevalent and where nothing remains of the Slavic but the names of cities, villages, and rivers."

It stands to reason that the language, returning to its own after a disuse of almost two hundred years and dug from the grave of oblivion, needed much burnishing, purifying, and modernizing. Terminology of arts and sciences, that flourished while the language lay dormant, had to be created. Dictionaries, grammars, and histories had to be compiled. Above all, the dross of alien forms had to be removed and, while the old Bohemian of Hus, Comenius, and Blahoslav constituted an inexhaustible store of material, it was necessary to borrow from kindred Slavic tongues and to coin many modern terms.

That the older writers composed some of their works in German seems paradoxical (German in these instances was used to defeat German), yet it was natural, considering the low state of Bohemian culture and the corresponding literary excellence in neighboring Germany. Thus, John Kollár, the apostle of literary Pan-Slavism, wrote his main work in German. Josef Dobrovský, already mentioned, composed all his works in German. Josef Šafařík's monumental volume on "Slavic Antiquities" was also written in German; even the "Father of his country," Francis Palacký, wrote his "History of the Bohemian Nation"[10] in the tongue of Schiller and Goethe. When, in 1831, a number of writers gathered in a well-known coffee-house in Prague, Čelakovský, one of them, remarked, half jokingly and half seriously, that Bohemian letters would perish should the ceiling of the room where they were chatting fall and kill those present.

The literary men and the "vlastenci" (patriots) were looked upon by many people with good-natured tolerance. Enemies of the cause regarded them with ill-concealed suspicion, not infrequently with contempt, while the government,

[10] See page 17.

distrusting everything that was new, suspected them of dangerous intrigues against the safety of the state. It must be borne in mind that there was no political freedom in Austria then; matters of public concern were not allowed to be discussed, much less criticised, except among intimates.

The work of resuscitating a dying race was a gigantic task, and but for the perseverance of the first apostles, the most promising branch of the Slavic linden tree would have withered. It was necessary to build theatres, to found learned societies, to establish museums and libraries, to collect and edit rare books and manuscripts scattered in foreign countries, whither they had been carried by soldiers during the Thirty Years' War. The Austrian Government, instead of assisting in this work which had for its object the uplifting of a down-trodden people from ignorance, superstition, and bigotry, hindered it at every step. As an example of self-sacrificing patriotism, the case of a law student by the name of Řehoř should be mentioned. This man took a vow that he would distribute as many Bohemian books as were said to have been burnt by the Jesuit Koniáš during the anti-reformation, that is, 60,000 volumes. Řehoř died some time in the late fifties of the nineteenth century, and he is said to have accomplished the greater part of his self-imposed task. When Jungmann, one of the greatest of the revivalists, died in 1847, the patriots had an opportunity to review their growing ranks and they were astonished how the national movement had spread. "When we were returning home from the funeral," noted J. V. Frič in his memoirs, "I walked arm in arm with my father; we both felt proud like victors who were marching to further decisive battles. When father in the evening sat down for a chat with the family, he exclaimed, breathing freely as if a stone had rolled off his chest, 'Children, I think we shall win; there are too many of us; they can no longer trample us down.'"

POLITICAL AWAKENING.

Up to 1848 Austrian subjects enjoyed certain liberties: they could smoke, drink, and play cards without interference from the police. One enjoyment, however, was denied to them—they were not permitted to think. Prince Metternich, the personification of absolutist Austria of those days, observed with alarm how the structure that he had been propping for years was beginning to settle in its foundations, and how ominous cracks appeared in it here and there.

Revolution was in the air. Switzerland, Germany, and Italy were being engulfed by it. "The world is ill," Metternich complained in a letter to Count Apponyi. "Each day we can observe how the moral infection is spreading, and if you find me unyielding, it is because I am of a nature that will not give in before opposition."

The news of the fall of Louis Philippe in France reached Prague February 29, 1848. Next day, notwithstanding the strictest censorship, the city was aflame with revolutionary talk. The liberals in neighboring Germany had summoned delegates to meet at Frankfort, March 5th. Italy seethed with political excitement. Kossuth, in Hungary, demanded that a constitution be granted to the people in Austria. Overnight Metternich's elaborate system of government, maintained by the police and the military, was tumbling down like a house of cards. In Prague, as in other large centres, everybody clamored for a constitution, though the masses, educated as they were to regard the government as something above and apart from them, hardly comprehended what the word "constitution" meant.

In the midst of the turmoil the sickly Emperor Ferdinand V. (1835-1848) abdicated in favor of his nephew, Francis Josef, then a youth of eighteen. The latter had been on the throne but a few weeks, when his advisers, Schwarzenberg, Windischgrätz, Stadion, and others, decided to do away with the constitution of the revolutionists and to substitute it with an octroy constitution, the reason assigned being "the incapacity of parliament." The choice fell on this particular young man because Prince Schwarzenberg recommended as ruler "one whom he would not have to be ashamed to show to the troops." Though not relevant, it is interesting to recall how the present emperor acquired his cognomen. "What shall it be, gentlemen," asked Schwarzenberg in the ministerial council—"Francis Josef, or simply Francis?" A sub-secretary of state thought that plain Francis would sound very well indeed, but the fear having been expressed that the name Francis might remind the Austrian nations too much of the ghost of Metternich, Francis Josef, instead of plain Francis, was chosen for the youthful monarch.

To Windischgrätz constitutions, ministries accountable to the people, and parliaments were abominations. He made no secret of the fact that he was opposed to the rule of lawyers; those alone who carried bayonets and muskets were entitled to be called patriots and saviors of the fatherland.

Under the Premiership of Alexander Bach (1853-1859) the monarchy relapsed to the methods of police rule that obtained prior to 1848. The reactionaries who surrounded the throne encouraged the youthful monarch to rule like an autocrat.

Minister Bach, by the way a highly gifted man, who had in his early days trifled with radicalism, believed that an alliance between the church and the state would strengthen both and that against the unity of the altar and the throne the radicals would be powerless. "The Austrian Monarchy," he confided to a noted clerical, "considering its peculiar structure, has only two firm bases on which it can rest in safety and unity,—the dynasty and the church." Accordingly he brought about, in 1855, the adoption of the famous concordat, a convention between the pope and the monarchy, a pact that increased immensely the legal power of the papacy in Austria. The concordat was abolished in 1868 because of the bitter opposition of the liberals. Bohemia, the land of Hus and Havlíček, fought the concordat openly and fearlessly, suspecting in it a hidden menace to its freedom of conscience and to national aspirations.

The uncompromising opposition of the Bohemians to Bach and to his policies visited upon them the wrath of Vienna. Under Bach they were probably subjected to oppression more ruthless and cruel than any they had experienced since the time of Ferdinand II.

Patriots, some of them mere youths, were thrown in prison on the flimsiest accusation of police spies. It was not safe to converse in Bohemian in the streets of Prague. Spies were at the heels of every Bohemian prominent in public life. Police agents tried to connect Francis L. Rieger with a treasonable plot to disrupt the monarchy and he had to flee the state to save himself from prison. Spies followed Palacký even to the sick-bed of his wife. The military authorities at Prague suspended the publication of Havlíček's famous newspaper, "Národní Noviny," on the ground that its editor indulged in "immoderate language." Finding Prague closed to his paper, Havlíček made an attempt to publish it in Vienna. "I am determined not to issue licenses to any newspaper in Vienna; we have enough newspapers as it is," replied General Welden to Havlíček's application for the license. "But there is no such newspaper in Vienna as I should like to publish," pleaded Havlíček. "My paper is intended to be an organ for Slavic matters and it is to be printed in Bohemian." Welden retorted angrily: "Wir sind hier Deutsche" (Here in Vienna we are Germans), and the General's decision was irrevocable.

Undaunted, Havlíček made other attempts to procure a newspaper license, and at last he obtained a promise that he might be allowed to publish a paper in Kutná Hora, a provincial town not far from Prague. In time even this paper was suppressed by the police and its editor arrested and interned in the province of Tyrol by Bach's order. It should, perhaps, be said that Havlíček was the one journalist whom neither threats nor offers of bribery could influence. There, separated from his wife and child, Havlíček gave way to brooding which brought on a fatal brain disease. From Tyrol he was permitted to return home, broken in health and spirit. To the last Havlíček remained steadfast to the cause he had championed—the liberation from bondage of his nation. Havlíček's colors were red and white (Bohemian national colors), and neither threats nor favors could swerve him from his chosen path:[11] "They banished you from the fatherland," wrote Pinkas to Havlíček, "but they transformed the fatherland itself into a fortress and a jail. We live here the most unhappy lives conceivable. Not a ray of light enters our intellectual prison to brighten it."

The mere acquaintanceship with Palacký was enough to expose one to the chicanery of the police. Strobach, at one time Mayor of Prague and a former speaker of the short-lived parliament, was deposed as judge because, when presiding at a trial, he failed to hold a drunkard on a charge of lèse majesté. Count Thun would not allow Rieger to lecture at the university for the reason, as he stated, "that students would see in him a political agitator, not a professor."

A demand was made on Palacký by the censor to strike out of his "History of the Bohemian Nation" the chapters relating to Hus and the Hussite Wars. Even Prince Metternich, whose bureaucratic leanings were above suspicion, considered the demand, which was equivalent to an order, unreasonable. After a great deal of haggling as to what was permissible and what should be deleted, a compromise was effected between the historian and the censor. However, Palacký's biogra-

---

[11] Karel Havlíček (1821-1856) is in many respects the most noteworthy Bohemian of the nineteenth century. As a journalist, he had no equal among his contemporaries. His political articles were models of sound and mature reasoning and of lucid thinking. When arguments failed with the black reactionaries, lay and ecclesiastic, Havlíček employed another weapon with telling effect—ridicule. Bohemians venerate him as a martyr of their cause. The cultured immigrants to the United States from Bohemia in the early days were imbued with Havlíček's spirit and ideas, and the present-day spread of free-thought among them is directly traceable to this Thomas Paine of Bohemia.

phers all agreed that the terms of the compromise were not satisfactory to him. He is said to have expressed a hope that future historians, living in freer times than he, should tell the whole truth about the importance and meaning of the Hussite movement, which he was not allowed to do. The chapters relating to the Hussite times he wrote both in Bohemian and German. But because German critics had impugned his impartiality, he determined, as a protest, to continue with Bohemian as the original and German as a translation. When he announced his decision to the Land Committee, a protest was raised and he was warned not to publish the Bohemian text before the German; nor to do anything from which it might appear that the German text was not the original.

The famous physician, Hamerník, a pupil of the noted Škoda and Rokytanský, was removed from the university because the government suspected his political and religious views.

The publication of every Bohemian newspaper in the land was suspended, except for two or three scientific and literary magazines, and the police would have liked to destroy even those, if decent pretext could have been found for their doing so.

At one time the authorities were planning to dissolve the society of the Bohemian Museum and the Royal Society of Sciences. The discussions of these learned bodies did not seem patriotic enough from the Austrian point of view. The Matice Česká—a society for the publication of standard literature—was threatened in its existence, and only the influence of some of its prominent members saved it from the fury of the almighty police.

Pogodin, the Russian scholar, had recommended the Matice to publish the works of Hus. "God prevent," answered Šafařík to Pogodin's letter (1857). "Who would think of publishing books on Hus in Austria?—yes, if they were against Hus—that would be simple."

Before Krejčí's work on geology could be published, every page, nay every line, was carefully scanned, and when that was done the manuscript was ordered to be submitted for approval to a learned priest, to make sure that it contained nothing contrary to the teaching of the church. Palacký, who was always dreaming of his pet scheme of the publication of a Bohemian encyclopedia, was told that "under the existing press laws it would be unwise to urge the matter."

In honor of the emperor's marriage (1854) the government showed clemency to certain political persons; yet, in general, conditions remained unchanged. Patriots who had been expelled from Prague could return, but city or country, their movements were watched by the police. Sladkovský, a famous journalist whose publications had been ruined by censorship, applied for a license to start a coal yard with which to support his family. The application was promptly disallowed. Young Frič, a literary rebel, planned to issue a volume of poetry with the collaboration of the younger set of writers. This warning was received from Vienna: "Let Frič beware; if he does not desist in his dangerous course, he may again find himself interned in a fortress." The police directors and press censors suspected the loyalty of everyone who ventured to write in Bohemian. "I fail to comprehend," remonstrated Police Director Weber with Frič, "why you persist in this ridiculous nonsense; in about six years there will be nothing left of your Bohemian literature, anyway."

On another occasion Weber gave Frič to understand that Bohemia was a German territory, and that if he wished to live in it he must obey German laws. Yet Frič was incorrigible. For his intractability and because he would not share Weber's view that his nation was doomed to extinction, he was banished to the hills of Transylvania.

On the battlefields at Magenta and Solferino in Italy in 1859, the absolutist rule of Bach, which derived its chief support from the bureaucracy, the military, and the clerical party, came to an abrupt end. The progressive element clamored for reforms. Bach was dismissed from office and his successor (Goluchowski) announced that in the future the state budget would be subject to the scrutiny of the people and that provincial diets would be invited to legislate on their needs. The last part of the program the federalists interpreted to mean that the principle of local self-government had at last been recognized.

In the Bohemian Diet a prominent member, encouraged by the program of the new premier, moved, amid genuine enthusiasm of the federalists, that a deputation of the diet be appointed to go to Vienna and urge the emperor to have himself crowned king in Prague. When, subsequently, a deputation of the diet secured an audience from the ruler, he declared (1861): "I will be crowned in Prague as King of Bohemia, and I am convinced that this ceremony will cement anew the indissoluble tie of confidence and loyalty between My throne and My Bohemian Kingdom."

Bohemians were elated. At last their ideal of autonomous Bohemia seemed at the point of realization.

Here a few words should be said concerning the constitution under which Austrians were to begin a new parliamentary life. The much-heralded and impatiently awaited document was drafted by Minister Schmerling, a staunch centralist, and because it was promulgated in February (1861) it was called the "Constitution of February." As soon as its text had been made public, the Slavs instantly recognized that the statesmen in Vienna had not profited in the slightest from the lessons of 1848. Minister Schmerling, was, like all Germans, obsessed with the notion that German hegemony was indispensable to the safety and greatness of the state. Accordingly he subordinated every other idea and interest to that one obsession. A most ingenious electoral system was evolved whereby Germans, though in minority, were able to control, not only the central parliament, but the provincial diets as well. The scheme was to favor the cities, wealthy individual taxpayers, and chambers of commerce (which groups then were German in sentiment) to the disadvantage of the agricultural districts inhabited by the Slavs. How the electoral law worked in Bohemia one can perceive from the fact that in 1873 2,500,000 Bohemians were able to elect only 34 deputies, while 1,500,000 Germans contrived to return 56 deputies. The powers of the provincial diets were reduced to a minimum, the controlling idea, of course, being to keep centred in Vienna the entire power of the state. By reason of this juggling the Bohemian element found itself in minority in its own Land Diet.

Although distrustful because of the partisanship evinced in the constitution, the Bohemians nevertheless entered parliament, but they did so upon the express understanding that their participation therein should not be in any manner prejudicial to the historical rights of their kingdom.

Generally speaking, the Austrian nations, from the very first day their representatives were permitted to enter the legislative halls, divided themselves into two political parties, federalists and centralists. The federalists favored granting self-government to the various races; the centralists, who were backed by the German masses, opposed this. Austria, according to the latter, was lost to the German cause the moment the agitation "Away from Vienna" had gained the upper hand. For reasons of self-protection the Slavs, led by the Bohemians, inclined toward federalism, as more likely to satisfy their national aspirations. Instead of a Teutonic Austria, the Slavs desired a United States of Austria that should be just and impartial to all.

For months the Bohemians waited, but to their surprise and dismay the government took no steps to make effective the emperor's promise. On the contrary, the increasing persecution of their press, the brutal partiality of the speaker of parliament, the hostile attitude of the executive organs of the government were signs, the significance of which could not be doubted. The discouraging truth dawned on them at last that the emperor had no intention of keeping his word and of giving home rule to his Bohemian subjects.

Deceived by their sovereign and realizing that neither reason nor justice would influence Vienna, they decided, in 1863, as a means of protest and to show their deep resentment, to leave the parliament in a body. On June 17th of that year they issued a statement in which the grievances of the nation were set forth at length. For sixteen years after that no Bohemian legislator appeared in the Austrian Parliament. And while this may not have been a sagacious course—indeed, subsequent events have shown that the "policy of abstinence," as the parliamentary boycott came to be known, almost irreparably prejudiced their position—yet, as a protest of an outraged nation, it was magnificent.

DUALISM—A BLUNDER AND A CRIME.

Up to 1867 the Hapsburg Monarchy was, outwardly at least, a Teutonic state. But in 1866, having been decisively beaten by Prussia at Sadova, it found itself facing a new destiny. Expelled from the Germanic Bund of which it had been a leading member, the championship wrested from it by victorious Hohenzollerns, rent by internal discord, its statesmen concurred in the opinion that reconstruction of some kind was inevitable. But what course of action should be pursued? Should the government again have recourse to the shop-worn policy of rigid centralization and Germanization which had been tried by Austrian Premiers time and time again and invariably found wanting?

That Hungary should be given back her autonomy was conceded beforehand.

Weakened by war, its military prestige shattered, its finances at a low ebb, the government was in no condition to resist the Magyars, who had assumed a threatening attitude. But what about the Bohemians, who also clamored for recognition? Bohemia, Hungary, and Austria, it will be remembered, had formed a union in 1526-1527 on terms of equality. And then how should the larger Slavic questions be settled? Numerically the Slavs were the strongest element in the monarchy. If allowed to elect representatives to one central parliament, these discontented Bohemians, Poles, Slovaks, and Croatians might one day, uniting politically, control the country. Tacitly Vienna and Budapest agreed that, whatever the terms of the settlement with Hungary, the disaster of Slavic majority must be averted.

"The Slavs must be pressed to the wall" (Man wird die Slaven an die Wand drücken), declared a statesman who participated actively in the plan of reconstruction. "You," addressing the Magyars, "will take care of your hosts [meaning the Slavs] and we shall take care of ours."

In the parliament the cause of the Slavic federalists was lost beforehand; a German-made constitution and German-made electoral law rendered futile every opposition. Besides, the government would brook no interference with its plan of reconstruction as outlined by Count Beust.[12] This plan contemplated a dual government, one in Vienna, the other in Budapest, and three parliaments, one to sit in Vienna for the Austrian half, one to meet in Budapest for the Hungarian half, and a third one to be called the "Delegations" and to convene alternately at both capitals to deliberate on matters common to the empire as a whole, such as foreign relations, the army, navy, finances, and so forth. In other words, Beust's plan provided for two seats of centralization instead of one. From a German state that it had been before 1867 Austria became a German-Magyar state—an organization without precedent or analogy.

The several kingdoms, crown-lands, etc., were divided under Beust's plan; and, upon the consummation of the deal, were allotted to the contracting parties to the dualism as follows: Austria received Bohemia, Moravia, Silesia, Bukovina, Dalmatia, Galicia, Carinthia, Carniola, Trieste and vicinity, Goritz and Gradiska, Istria, Lower Austria, Upper Austria, Salzburg, Styria, Tyrol, Voralberg. Hungary secured as her part of the bargain Hungary Proper, Transylvania, Fiume, Croatia, Slavonia, and the Military Frontier.

Figures, better than anything else, will explain why the Slavs were opposed to dualism and presently became its irreconcilable enemies. Under the Austrian roof Beust put these Slavic groups (quoting from the census of 1910):

---

[12] Friedrich Ferdinand Beust, a Saxon statesman, entered the services of Austria soon after the disaster at Sadova. It was he who brought to a successful termination the Settlement between Vienna and Hungary. The centralists were at first opposed to the division of Austria in two, but were eventually placated by Beust, he having convinced them that dualism meant the permanent subjugation of the Slavs. The above remark, "Die Slaven werden an die Wand gedrückt," is attributed to him.

Bohemians	6,435,983
Poles	4,967,984
Slovenes	1,252,940
Serbo-Croatians	783,334
Little Russians	3,608,844
Total	17,049,085

Under the Magyar domination fell the following Slavs:

Slovaks	1,967,970
Croatians	1,833,167
Serbs	1,106,471
Little Russians	472,587
	5,380,195

Beust's scheme was audaciously clever. By dividing the monarchy in two he divided the Slavs; and, separated and isolated, they were made easier victims of Magyarization in Hungary and of Germanization in Austria. A crying injustice of this shameful bargain was that the "high contracting parties" tore apart peoples of the same race, setting up a political barrier where nature intended that none should exist. Austria, for instance, had been awarded Dalmatia, the population of which is almost wholly Croatian; yet Slavonia and Croatia, which is also Croatian to the core (or Serbo-Croatian), went to Hungary. Bohemians of Bohemia, Moravia, and Silesia were lodged under the Austrian roof; the Slovaks, on the other side, who are almost one with the Bohemian race, were put under the guardianship of Hungary. Nations and races were moved on the Austrian chess-board like so many pawns—exactly the same way as at the Vienna Congress in 1814 and at the Berlin Conference in 1878.

"No people in the monarchy were more unjustly prejudiced by dualism than the Bohemians," is the opinion of Denis. "Every article of the Settlement affected their interests most adversely. Their kinsmen, the Croatians and Serbs, and particularly the Slovaks—the latter always confidently looked upon as a reserve force of the nation—were handed out to merciless and unfeeling masters. The crown of St. Václav (St. Václav is honored as patron saint of Bohemia) was reduced by Vienna to a position of semi-vassalage and given equal rank with a medley of outlying and insignificant provinces. Dualism condemned the Slavs to be the unwilling tools of a policy to which they had been opposed. Bohemia, the richest and most productive land in the empire, was made to bear the heaviest quota of the burden with which statesmen had saddled the Austrian half of the monarchy." Condemning dualism, Dr. Edward Grégr, in a famous speech delivered in parliament, declared "that it would be wisest to tear down to its foundations the ramshackle building that made every tenant dissatisfied, that lacked light and air, that neither expense nor labor could make habitable, and to build upon the ruins an edifice answering the manifold needs of its inhabitants. In the judgment of Dr. Menger" (a German deputy), thundered Grégr, "this would be a treason and I confess that it would be a treason. Yet, is not dualism a treason on the rights and liberties of the peoples of this state and particularly on the rights and liberties of our Bohemian nation?"

And because the settlement between Austria and Hungary had been effected without the co-operation, much less the consent of the Bohemians, whose claims were utterly disregarded—it will be remembered that at that time, 1867, they were boycotting the parliament—a series of political duels were fought between Vienna and Prague, which in the end resulted in the defeat of the weaker antagonist, that is, Prague.

In the spring of 1867 the Prague Diet was summoned to elect deputies to the parliament which was to vote on the settlement with Hungary. The Bohemians refused to elect such deputies and entered instead a vigorous protest against being incorporated in Austria-Hungary, then in process of formation. The only state they recognized was the Bohemian Kingdom and this had as much right to autonomy as Hungary. Promptly the government dissolved the diet and ordered new elections. At these elections, thanks to the ingenious electoral law, the Bohemians were defeated and the German minority, now master in the diet, proceeded to elect delegates to the Vienna Parliament. The Bohemians declared this election unconstitutional and fraudulent. Deputies so elected, they maintained, were not true representatives of the people and could not, therefore, legally or morally bind the nation in parliament. Having issued this protest, the Bohemians left the diet, and the next year, instead of returning, issued their memorable Declaration of Rights, bearing date August 22, 1868. They continued to boycott the Land Diet until 1870.

The government was by no means tardy in making the rebels feel that they needed to be disciplined for their refusal to participate in the labors of the parliament. The Director of Police in Prague received orders to see to it "that Bohemian newspapers moderate their tone." That, of course, meant the inevitable lawsuits, police chicanery, confiscation, fines, jail.

To break the rebellious spirit of the Bohemians the government sent Baron Koller to Prague, as Military Governor,—a soldier of the Radecký type of Austrian generals—brutal, violent. One of his first acts was to place the capital under martial law (1868). Koller suspended the publication of nearly every Bohemian newspaper. Arrests for political crimes became so numerous that the jail of the New Town (one of the Boroughs of Prague) held at one time 400 prisoners, though there was room only for 250 persons. During 1868 in Prague alone Koller sent to jail 144 persons who were convicted of political misdemeanors and crimes. The total penalties aggregated 81 years. How many prisoners there were in the provincial towns in Bohemia and Moravia is only conjectured, but it was asserted afterwards that there had been five times as many as in Prague, so that the total number of political prisoners in Bohemia in 1868 was about 700.

When the Premier tried to placate the Bohemian opposition by suspending martial law (April, 1869) in Prague, the centralists became furious. Bohemian autonomy, declared their organ, the Vienna "Neue Freie Presse," is an issue that only force can solve; the unification of the Bohemian Crown may be of vital moment to the Bohemians, but the Germans will never give their consent.

FRANCIS JOSEF, A WORD-BREAKER.

At last wiser counsel prevailed in Vienna, and while certain members favored repression, even force, to bring the Bohemians to submission, there were others, Count Taaffe among them, who urged moderation. The Potocki ministry (1870) tried to breach the differences between Prague and Vienna. More successful than Potocki was Count Hohenwart, whom the emperor encouraged to make terms with the Bohemians. Hohenwart's first step was to name two distinguished Bohemians, Jireček and Habětínek, members of his cabinet. The "Neue Freie Presse" commented on Hohenwart's appointment as "the Sedan of German ideals in Austria." Hohenwart's next step was to select an Austrian commission, in co-operation with a similar commission of Bohemians, headed by Count Clam-Martinic and Dr. Rieger, to draft terms of settlement, which came to be known as the "Fundamental Articles." These "Fundamentals" defined precisely the future relations of Bohemia and Austria. In the "Fundamentals" one could clearly discern Palacký's ideas of federalistic Austria.

Thereupon an imperial rescript was issued, bearing date September 12, 1871, in which the emperor made this memorable promise: "Recognizing the state rights of the Bohemian Crown, calling to mind the renown and power which the crown has conferred upon Us and Our predecessors, and mindful further of the unwavering loyalty with which the people of Bohemia have at all times supported Our throne, We are glad to recognize the rights of this kingdom and are ready to renew this recognition by Our coronation oath."[13]

Obviously it was not the mere mediæval ceremony of coronation that Bohemians were anxious to have take place. By having himself crowned as king, the sovereign would affirm by implication that the Kingdom of Bohemia, the Margravate of Moravia, and the Duchy of Silesia were one and indivisible; that Bohemia was a part of the monarchy only as long as the Hapsburgs survived in the male or female line; that in the event of the Hapsburg-Lothringen line becoming extinct, Bohemia was free to elect its own ruler; that the power of legislation was vested jointly in the king and in the diets and that the king, upon taking the coronation oath, bound himself to defend the indissolubility of the Bohemian Crown.

In answer to the emperor's declaration the diet passed in its sessions of October 8 and 10, 1871, the "Fundamental Articles." Meantime the centralists worked indefatigably to defeat the settlement with Bohemia. Their journals employed ev-

---

[13] "Eingedenk der Staatsrechtlichen Stellung der Krone Böhmens und des Glanzes und der Macht bewusst, welche dieselbe Uns und Unseren Vorfahren verliehen hat, eingedenk ferner der unerschütterlichen Treue, mit welchen die Bevölkerung Böhmens jederzeit Unseren Thron stützte, erkennen wir gerne die Rechte dieses Königreiches an und sind bereit diese Anerkennung mit Unserem Krönungseide zu erneuern."

Among the many titles of Francis Josef are those of "Emperor of Austria," "King of Hungary," "King of Bohemia," etc. Strictly speaking, Francis Josef has no legal claim to the title "King of Bohemia." He has never taken the coronation oath; and, without such an oath, he is no more King than Woodrow Wilson would be President of the United States without first taking the oath of office. Logically, therefore, Francis Josef is an unlawful ruler of the Bohemian Kingdom.

ery means to prejudice public opinion against it. "Austria is about to capitulate to the Slavs," wrote these journals, "and Prague will eventually supersede Vienna as the capital of the empire."

It is known that Bismarck, fearing that Bohemian home rule might have a stimulating effect on his Poles, and Andrassy, solicitous about the "welfare" of his Slovaks, jointly intrigued to defeat the autonomy which Premier Hohenwart was ready to concede. "Hungary will have nothing in common with Slavic Austria," declared the "Pester Lloyd," speaking for the Hungarian Government. "We Hungarians shall do everything in our power to frustrate the reconstruction. Call it selfishness, if you will, but that shall be our policy."

The victory of the Prussians over the French in 1871 naturally made the Austro-German centralists more stubborn than ever, and Hohenwart, despairing of the passage in the parliament of the "Fundamental Articles," resigned October 30th. For the second time since 1848 the rehabilitation of the Bohemian State had been frustrated. That the emperor, always vacillating and ever fearful of the Pan-Germans, was not himself without blame, is obvious. In fact, it is charged that the coterie of archdukes around the throne welcomed opposition to Bohemian home rule, if it did not secretly foment it.

A new rescript commanded the diet to elect delegates to the parliament. Refusing to do this, the diet was dissolved. The Auersperg-Lasser Ministry which followed Hohenwart was outspokenly German-centralistic and Bohemian autonomists made ready for another onslaught from Vienna.

NEW PERSECUTIONS.

For the second time the "opposition tamer," Baron Koller, was appointed Governor of Bohemia. To Moravia was sent the notorious Bohemiophobe, Baron Weber. As usual, the press was the first to feel the heel of these little despots. Public prosecutors throughout Bohemia and Moravia received instructions to proceed "fearlessly" against opposition journals. Those prosecutors who replied that they would do their duty strictly "in accordance with the law" were either removed or transferred to other posts and replaced by functionaries who were more mindful of the needs of the government. "It is not necessary in every instance to set forth the reason for the confiscation of a newspaper article," the prosecutors were instructed. "The prosecutors have a full power to act and they are answerable to no one." During the first year of the Auersperg-Lasser Ministry the daily newspaper "Politik" in Prague was confiscated 83 times by the conscientious prosecutor. A number of societies were dissolved, though non-political in character. An agricultural organization that had been founded during the reign of Maria Theresa and had survived the bitter days of Bach's administration, was deprived of its charter because its president, Prince Charles Schwarzenberg, a Bohemian noble, declined to participate in the Vienna Exposition unless a separate space was allotted there to Bohemia, as to Hungary. Every presiding officer of the so-called District Committees in the provinces, who was suspected of being a Bohemian sympathizer, was summarily removed. Two of the most noted journalists, Julius Grégr and J. St. Skrejšovský, who had the courage to fight the Auersperg-Lasser Ministry openly, were put in jail for an alleged attempt to defraud the government of a trifling tax with which newspaper advertisements were assessable. Both languished in jail for months. As an instance of official meanness, the case of the publisher of the "Correspondence Slave" should be mentioned. This man received a long term in prison for failure to pay a newspaper tax amounting to less than half a florin (20 cents).

And because Bohemian juries almost uniformly acquitted journalists brought before them for political offenses, prosecuting attorneys resorted to the expedient of a change of venue to cities inhabited by Germans. To eminent jurists protesting that a procedure of this kind was unconstitutional, the Minister of Justice replied that state necessities justified this course. On one occasion a deputation of representative citizens of Prague called on Baron Koller to complain of the arbitrariness of the police. "Gentlemen, I hope you do not wish me to be uncivil to you. I am exceedingly busy, and inasmuch as I have nothing to say to you, I must ask you to leave the room in five minutes." And when the deputation, incensed over Koller's brusqueness, wished to explain, the redoubtable baron exclaimed: "Gentlemen, the five minutes are up. Leave." A door was opened, and in the ante-room stood a sentry with fixed bayonet.

The year 1879 witnessed the end of the "policy of abstinence." Due, largely, to Premier Taaffe's persuasion and promises, Bohemians re-entered the parliament. From Taaffe and his successors in office they obtained some political concessions (crumbs fallen from the opulent table of the master, to repeat a current expression of the opposition), yet the supreme ideal of the nation, autonomy, is to-day no nearer fulfillment than it ever was. If they thought that they might be able to convince Vienna of the injustice of dualism and might by parliamentary pressure force it to grant to them home rule of which they had been twice cheated, they had reckoned wrongly. Not only did they fail to bring Vienna to terms, but they were made to feel that another foe, powerful and implacable, blocked their way to national freedom. That foe was Berlin. For it must not be forgotten that, since the formation of the Triple Alliance, Berlin influence at Vienna, always great, had become predominant. If the two Teutonic partners were agreed on any one thing, it was on the proposition that Slavic trees in Austria should not grow too tall.

To conduct the reader through the maze of purely local happenings that occurred since Taaffe's administration would be a long, though not wholly uninteresting story. Suffice it to say that during most of the time Bohemians were forced to fight on two fronts—Vienna on one front and their fellow-countrymen with Pan-German leanings on the other. The main quarrel between Vienna and Prague during all these years has been over Home Rule. Shall Bohemians living in the countries comprising the Bohemian Crown (Bohemia, Moravia, Silesia) be the arbiters of their own destiny, and shall they govern themselves from Prague by laws made and enacted by their home parliament? Home Rule is and has been the main issue; all else is subordinate to it.

WAR WITHOUT SANCTION OF PARLIAMENT.

In 1908 the German minority in the Bohemian Diet proposed a plan aiming at a division of Bohemia into two administrative parts, German and Bohemian. This plan the Bohemians vehemently combated, as they had consistently opposed like schemes in the past. They claimed that to rend the kingdom into two halves, Bohemian and German, was both impracticable and dangerous. Impracticable, because it would condemn to inevitable Germanization the very strong Bohemian minorities living in German districts on the border. Dangerous, because there were good reasons for believing that German Bohemia would gravitate toward Berlin, rather than toward Prague or Vienna. Their scheme having been blocked, the Germans availed themselves of obstructive tactics in the diet, with the result that a deadlock ensued. As usual, the Vienna Government hurried to the assistance of the Germans. Bohemian leaders were made to understand that they must yield in the Prague Diet, or suffer punishment in the parliament. However, neither threats nor promises moved the Bohemians; they made it plain that they would not submit to further political extortions. Unable to break the deadlock in Bohemia and unwilling to abandon the Germans in their hopeless struggle for the maintenance of Teutonic hegemony in Austria, the Vienna Government, as a last desperate means of saving its compatriots from political defeat, suspended what there was still left of Bohemian autonomy on July 26, 1913, one year before the outbreak of the war, having previously advised the Berlin Government of its intention. The diet was dissolved, although new elections had not been ordered, as the law provided, and in place of the autonomous Land Executive, the government appointed an Imperial Commission to govern Bohemia. This was the beginning of an absolutist era in the kingdom.

The echo of the deadlock in Bohemia was at once heard in parliament. Promptly the Bohemians carried the fight to the imperial assembly, thus crippling its functions. And so it happened that, on the eve of the Great War, the highest legislative tribunal of the empire did not meet and the nations were not consulted as to whether or not they wished war. The ruler alone decided this momentous question by taking recourse to the famous paragraph fourteen of the constitution which, in certain cases, allows him to act alone without the co-operation or advice of the parliament.[14] This situation really suited the wishes of the government

[14] The elusive paragraph fourteen of the constitution (bearing date December 21, 1867) has been the cause of some of the bitterest fights in parliament. It virtually nullifies constitutionalism in Austria, permitting as it does the emperor and his ministers to rule the land "in case of urgent necessities" without parliament. Past experience has shown that these "necessities" arise quite often. Paragraph fourteen is a bulwark of strength to the German party against which the Bohemians have battled in vain. Under paragraph fourteen the ruler cannot change the fundamental laws of the realm, contract permanent loans, and alienate public property. Aside from this there is nothing to curb his absolutism. Parliament may impeach the ministers for exceeding their powers, but this safeguard is really no safeguard at all. The German text of paragraph fourteen is as follows:

"Wenn sich die dringende Nothwendigkeit solchen Anordnungen, zu welchem verfassungsmässig die Zustimmung des Reichsrathes erforderlich ist, zu einer Zeit herausstellt, wo dieser nicht versammelt ist, so können dieselben unter Verantwortung des Gesammtministeriums durch Kaiserliche Verordnung erlassen werden, in soferne solche keine Abänderung des Staatsgrundgesetzes bezwecken, keine dauernde Belastung des Staatschatzes, und keine Veräuserung von Staatsgut betreffen. Solche Verordnungen haben provisorische Gesetzkraft, wenn sie von sämmtlichen Ministern unterzeichnet sind, und mit

clique, which knew beforehand that the Slavs would have resolutely opposed the war if given an opportunity. Certain it is that the Bohemians would have raised their voice against the mad adventure against Serbia and would have declared in no unequivocal language that a ruler who had twice broken his solemn promise to them had little claim on their loyalty.

In a hundred different ways the nation is being wronged and held back, and no lasting relief is possible so long as the deadening centralistic, anti-Slavic policy obtains, so long as the state recognizes master races and servant races and accords different treatment to each.

To every one of its political and cultural demands Vienna is ready to plead reasons of state, policies of state, principles of state, necessities of state. If the grumbling is too loud the malcontents are given to understand: "If you are not satisfied in Austria, you may have a chance to become Prussians."

"Our nation is in a grave danger," said Palacký, "and surrounded on all sides by enemies. Yet I believe that it will conquer in the end, if it is only determined." And the Bohemian nation is determined, determined to the last man, to fight for its life, its liberty, and its happiness.

HAPSBURGS DISTRUSTED.

If there is one thing deeply rooted in the minds of the Bohemian people it is the belief, or rather the conviction, that the Hapsburgs, beginning with Ferdinand II. and ending with Francis Josef, the present sovereign, one and all planned the Germanization of the nation. Vienna newspapers make much of the fact that Bohemia has advanced under the rule of Francis Josef as under no other Hapsburg—and they seek to convey the impression that this remarkable renascence should be credited to his reign. If Francis Josef had had his way, Bohemians argue, they would to-day be like the Slavs along the Elbe who have succumbed to Germanization, and Prague would be as German as Leipzig or Vienna. Their own determination to live saved them from extinction. All that the nation is and all that it has attained it has accomplished through its own effort, without help from Vienna, often in the face of the bitterest opposition from that quarter. Deny it as much as you will, the truth remains that Bohemians, remembering their experience with Ferdinand II., have always distrusted the Hapsburgs; and Francis Josef has done nothing, despite the splendid opportunities of his remarkably long reign, to dispel that feeling of distrust. For, who was it but a Hapsburg who, in the first half of the seventeenth century, turned their fatherland into a waste, driving into exile the flower of the nation? Who but a Hapsburg put a tombstone on the sepulchre of the nation, and who but a Hapsburg tried to smother its spirit under that tombstone? Who but a Hapsburg caused the persecution and jailing of the revivalists who undertook the task of awakening the nation? And who but a Hapsburg twice violated, twice broke his solemn promise to the nation, first in 1861, and again in 1871? Who but a Hapsburg, by approving of the dualistic system of government in 1867, <u>intrigued to barter them away, with the rest of the Slavs, into political</u> bondage?

ausdrücklicher Beziehung auf diese Bestimmung des Staatsgrundgesetzes kundgemacht werden."

LOYALTY AND UNITY.

Reading the utterances of Austrian officials in the United States one is almost persuaded to believe that the reports of mutinies in the early stages of the war and of disaffection of Slavic troops were pure inventions of a hostile press, that the nations in the Hapsburg Monarchy were enthusiastic and united[15] on the question of war and that stories of oppression of non-Germanic peoples were baseless, lacking the foundation of truth. A member of one of the consular staffs made a pretty speech before the New York Twilight Club in which he tried to convince his hearers that it was an old-time policy of the Austrian Government to treat justly and impartially all its subjects, irrespective of race, for does not the Hofburg in Vienna, the residence of the emperor, bear the proud legend, "Justice to all nations is the fundament of Austria"?

Is it really true that the Austrian troops are and were loyal, that none shot their officers and none surrendered to the Russians or to the Serbians when an opportunity presented? Do not these very denials of mutiny and disaffection sound suspicious? Mutiny of troops is admittedly unknown in the German Army, and none have been, so far as we know, reported from the French or English Armies. Neither the Germans, nor the English, nor the French officials in this country have felt the need to make public affirmation or denial where silence should have been most eloquent. If the Austro-Hungarian officials are so sure of their case, why do they make an exception and try to refute what in the case of the other warring countries is understood as a matter of course?

Before we could give unreserved credence to these official assurances, we should like to hear the other side of the story. But, it so happens that the other side cannot now be presented. Every newspaper in Austria, without an exception (particularly opposition journals printed in any of the Slavic languages), is edited by the government. The government censor is editor of all journals published in the empire, and the newspapers are given the choice either to print what the Imperial Royal Press Bureau sends them or have the articles promptly confiscated. As a result of this complete muzzling of the press, there is now but one kind of public opinion in Austria—the censor's opinion. According to the Prague journals, which reach the United States, Austrians are winning everywhere—on land, at sea, and in the air. Police agents plan fraternal and loyal meetings of Germans and Slavs, and the police agents' faithful ally, the censor, writes them up in the newspapers and the Imperial Royal Press Bureau in Vienna sends broadcast glowing accounts of them. Again, many of the leading men of the Bohemian nation are in jail or under strict police surveillance and cannot speak. Are we to believe that all the Austrian races fight enthusiastically? Precisely the opposite of this is true. With the exception of a fraction of the Galician Poles, the Slavs were entirely opposed

---

[15] The register of prisoners at Kiev shows 114,000 were taken in the Carpathian fighting during the two months before the fall of Przemysl, and some difficulty has been found in preventing racial troubles among the enormous colony from captives. German Uhlan soldiers, hearing of the fall of Przemysl, declared that it must have been due to the treachery of "that Czech Kusmanek," whereupon a Czech officer struck him. The fight spread and the participants had to be separated.—*Cable item from Russia.*

to the war with Serbia.[16] Unfortunately they have no voice in the foreign policy of

[16] The Slavs in Austria-Hungary are divided into the following racial groups:

1. *The Bohemians.* Inhabit Bohemia, Moravia, and Silesia. Strong settlements are found in Austria (the city of Vienna alone being the home of not less than 300,000, according to some estimates 500,000) and in Prussian Silesia.

2. *The Slovaks.* Settled in the northwestern part of Hungary and in Moravia.

Professor Lubor Niederle, who is recognized as an authority on Slavic matters, computed in 1900 the strength of the Bohemians, together with the Slovaks, at 9,800,000.

3. *The Poles.* Scattered over the whole of Galicia, intermixing there with the Ruthenes, but predominating mainly in the westerly part of it. They also live in Silesia, with settlements in Bukovina and Moravia. Austrian Poles number almost 5,000,000. All told, the Polish race in Austria, Germany, and Russia is computed by Niederle (1900) at 17,500,000; Polish statisticians make the total 20,000,000. When the constitutional era first dawned in Austria, the Poles were put in full charge of Galicia, in appreciation of which concession they have always loyally supported the Austrian Government. In Galicia, the Poles are the aristocracy and the Ruthenes the peasant element. The affection of Vienna for the Poles, however, is not above suspicion; it is claimed that hatred of Russia, common to both the Poles and the Austrians, was more directly responsible for the alliance than any other single cause, though of course it is undeniable that under Austrian rule the Poles fared better than either under the Russian or Prussian régimes.

4. *The Slovenes.* Occupy the whole of Carniola, the southern part of Styria, the major section of Goritz and Gradiska, except a section in the southwestern part thereof, the outlying villages of Trieste, the northern end of Istria, which projects on the west into Italian territory and eastward into Hungary. Niederle's estimate of the Slovenes in 1900 was 1,500,000.

5. No Slavic race is more torn up territorially than the *Serbo-Croatians.* Although really one people by language and origin, they have divided themselves, or rather were subdivided by their political masters, into two national units. Their homelands include a large section of Istria and Dalmatia, together with the adjacent islands in the Adriatic, the whole of Croatia and Slavonia, a piece of southern Hungary, and all of Bosnia and Herzegovina. Besides this, there is, of course, the Serbian Kingdom and Montenegro.

Niederle estimated the Serbo-Croatians in 1900 at 8,550,000.

6. *The Ruthenes* (Little Russians). Overflow the Russian boundaries to Galicia, being predominant in east Galicia, strong in western and northern Bukovina, numerous in several counties in Hungary.

Niederle computed the strength of the Ruthenes in Galicia, Hungary, and Bukovina in 1900 at 3,500,000.

By religious affiliations the Slavs are divided as follows: To the Catholic group belong almost wholly the Bohemians, Poles, Slovenes, Croatians, and Slovaks (of the last named about seven-tenths). Protestantism finds favor among the Slovaks (24 per cent.), Bohemians (2.44 per cent.), and Poles living in Silesia (1.81 per cent.). The Orthodox faith is professed by the Ruthenes in Galicia, Hungary, and Bukovina, and the Serbians. A fraction of the Russians in Galicia and Hungary adheres to the Uniate Church, and there are believers in Mohammedanism in Bosnia and Herzegovina.

The old-fashioned Austrian diplomacy knew well the value of the principle "divide and rule" and tried it on its Slavs with success. There was a time when Bohemians in Moravia were taught by Austrian officials to believe that they were Moravians, not Bohemians. The difference between Bohemian and Moravian is as great as the difference between

the monarchy; if their warnings and pleadings, as reflexed in their press, had been heeded, war against Serbia would never have been undertaken. Slavs are battling under the Austro-Hungarian standards because they cannot help themselves. Yet their hearts are not in the fight. Even the dullest and least informed mind will guess, notwithstanding the honeyed assurances of consular officials, the way their sympathies incline. It should be borne in mind that this is a war of Slavs against Slavs, of Slavic Russia and Slavic Serbia against two-fifths Slavic Austria. Let us place ourselves in the position of the Bohemians. For decades they have worked for solidarity among the Slavs, so much so that their endeavors in this direction have earned for them the title of the Apostles of Pan-Slavism. Is it reasonable to suppose that they would suddenly turn traitors to one of the most cherished traditions of their race and shout enthusiastically for a war which, if successful for the two Kaisers, would mean their certain obliteration? If Germany should win, the eventual absorption by her of Austria would be probable, if not inevitable. The Pan-German sentiment in the two neighboring empires would become so overwhelmingly strong that nothing would stay its furor and the millions of Austrian Slavs would find themselves face to face with their doom. Plainly, Slavs have nothing to gain from the defeat of the Allies, but everything to lose from the victory of the Hapsburgs and the Hohenzollerns. They feel that nothing short of a decisive defeat of Austria will liberate them from the thraldom of German-Magyar domination. If Austria collapses in this war the Bohemians will be among the first to profit thereby.[17]

Bronx English and Brooklyn English, yet this fact did not discourage the grammarians in Vienna from setting up boundaries where none existed. Croatia, as pointed out elsewhere, is peopled by a nation calling itself alternately Croatians and Serbs. Possessing a common past, the same racial traditions, and speaking one language, the Serbo-Croatians are clearly one nation, divided only by different faiths. The Croatians use the Latin letters and adhere, almost to a man, to the Catholic faith, while the Serbs employ the Cyrillic alphabet and belong to the Orthodox Church. The busy grammarians in Vienna and in Budapest did their utmost to keep the Serbo-Croatians apart, and even incited one against the other, by instilling the belief in them that two different religions really meant two different races. Galicia is inhabited by two distinct peoples, the Russians and the Poles. The name "Russian" sounded badly in Austria. It constantly reminded the Galician Russians that on the other side of the yellow-black boundary posts lived a great nation that spoke the same language and professed the same faith as they. Again the learned grammarians in Vienna went to work and by dint of hard study discovered that Austrian Russians were really not what they seemed to be and promptly they baptized them "Ruthenes." The ruse, of course, was to veil the nearness of the relationship of the "Ruthenes" to the Russians in Russia proper. In the same manner and with the same object in view the Slovaks of Hungary are encouraged to believe that they are a separate race and not near relatives of the Bohemians.

[17] For a student of Austrian conditions it is instructive to note how the war of the Balkan Allies against the Turk divided the sympathies of the people along racial lines. Save a fraction of the Poles in Galicia, the Slavs sided heartily and enthusiastically with the Allies. The Germans and the Magyars wished for the success of the Turks. When the Bulgars routed the Ottoman army at Kirk Killisé, the Vienna press ill-concealed its chagrin, while Slavic journals rejoiced as if it had been their own victory. Imagine the dismay of such a staunch champion of Austrian public opinion as the Vienna "Neue Freie Presse," when the Serbs crushed the Turk at Kumanovo! For many reasons Serbia was for years looked upon as a kind of barometer of the hopes of the Austrian Slavs. A clever Bohemian journalist made

Is it really true that the Slavs are loyal? Is it not rather a loyalty wrung from them at the point of the bayonet? Besides, how can they protest against a war which was neither of their choosing nor of their making, when the military rule has made protests impossible? One must respect and even admire the French and the Germans when they declare that they are fighting for the existence of the fatherland. What are the Austrian Slavs fighting for? To them, or rather to the majority of them, Austrian fatherland conveys but an abstraction, for correctly speaking, Austria is a government and not a fatherland in the sense that a German or a Frenchman regards the country of his birth. Austria may possibly be a fatherland to the inhabitants of the Archduchies of Lower and Upper Austria, but not to a Bohemian, a Magyar, or a Pole—certainly no more than England is the fatherland of an Irishman. By allegiance a Bohemian is an Austrian subject, ethnically he belongs to the country of his birth—Bohemia. While the national anthem "Kde domov můj" (Where is my Home?) stirs deeply the emotions of a Bohemian, the singing of the Austrian hymn "Gott erhalte" leaves him cold and indifferent.

VIENNA, THE CAPITAL.

Vienna loves to pose as the beacon-light of the empire somewhat as Paris, the recognized centre of everything French, or Berlin, the pivotal city of Germany. Yet Vienna forgets that it lacks all of the historical, geographical, economic essentials of Paris and, for that matter, of Berlin. What is Vienna? The residence of the sovereign and the seat of the government and the capital—not of the empire, mind you, but of the Archduchy of Lower Austria. The capital of Hungary is Budapest; the centre of attraction of the Poles is Cracow; the heart of the Bohemians is Prague. What has been the attitude of Vienna toward the non-German peoples and their national needs? The good-natured Viennese has for decades seen the Slavs caricatured on the stage, or in the humorous journals, as hopeless simpletons, while the Bohemian Wenzel was chosen by common consent as the quintessence of stupidity.

Several years ago a Bohemian Bank purchased palatial quarters on a leading thoroughfare, but it had to cover with cloth a Bohemian sign on the building until the municipality gave its consent thereto. A few years ago a company of actors, attached to the National Theatre at Prague, arranged to give in Vienna representative plays. Anti-Bohemian demonstrations, ending in riots, were the result.

Vienna, the capital of an empire that is inhabited by a dozen different races, and which counts among its inhabitants upward of 300,000 Bohemians, objected to a business sign in Bohemian, because it might mar the beauty of its looks as a German city! A few years ago the municipality ordered the closing of the Komenský Bohemian elementary school, ostensibly because it failed to comply with building and health ordinances. The real reason, however, was known to be political and

---

the interesting prediction some time before the Balkan War that relief from Austrian thraldom may be looked for, not from Russia, as many dreamers believed, but from the small Slavic states in the Balkans. If these were victorious, prophesied this newspaper writer, the Slavs in the Hapsburg Monarchy were sure to gain morally from the victory. Official public opinion frowned on the war relief work among Austrian Slavs in aid of the Balkan Allies.

racial antipathy. Is it any wonder, then, that the sentiment "Away from Vienna" is strong and that it grows stronger every year among non-Germans? "Vienna has always been to us," remarked a noted Bohemian writer, "a cruel, unforgiving step-mother."

THE PROBLEM.

On the surface the Austrian problem appears to be quite complicated, yet with the assistance of a few facts and figures much that is puzzling to casual observers becomes intelligible, if not perfectly clear.

Like most industrial countries, Austria is plagued with issues which follow in the wake of modernism—whatever that term may imply. Modernism there pounds with ever-increasing violence at the doors of the palaces of the opulent captains of industry. The small farmer is land-hungry. Industrialism has everywhere created new sources of wealth, yet with every factory erected or a mine opened the socialists have added so much to their disaffected ranks. A bitter war is being waged in certain sections of the monarchy between the clericals and the modernists, for it must not be forgotten that Austria is still a faithful daughter of Rome. If there are those who favor the "Los von Rom"—"Away from Rome"—movement, there are others who firmly believe that a steadfast loyalty to a faith different from that professed by the Prussian neighbor, really constitutes one of the most effective barriers against the ever-threatening absorption of Austria by Prussia.

Most important of all the problems, however, which confront Austria is that of nationalism. Nationalism was unknown to Austria in the days of Napoleon. Prior to 1848 Hapsburgs knew and recognized Austrian-Germans only. After that revolutionary year they were compelled to take notice, unwillingly enough, we may be sure, of other races. Bohemians, Magyars, Croatians, and others forced themselves to the front; and, resenting the broad and ethnically meaningless term "Austrian," demanded to be called by their proper racial names.

The voice that extolled racial patriotism had first been heard across the Austrian frontier from Frankfort, Germany, in 1848, when a parliament that had been summoned to that city called on Germans to unite. Promptly the Slavs took up the idea of unity and as a retaliatory measure summoned a Pan-Slavic Congress to meet in Prague. It was on the occasion of the Prague Congress that Francis Palacký addressed his famous letter to the Frankfortists, explaining why the Bohemians and other Slavs were opposed to the incorporation of Austria in the future Germany. "The aim which you propose to yourselves," wrote Palacký, among other things, to Frankfort, "is the substitution of a federation of peoples for the old federation of princes, to unite the German nation in a real union, to strengthen the sentiment of German nationality, to secure the greatness of Germans without and within. I honor your resolve and the motives by which you are impelled, but at the same time I cannot share in your work. I am not a German, or at least I do not feel as if I were one. Assuredly you cannot wish that I should join you merely as a supernumerary with neither opinion nor will of my own. I am a Bohemian of Slavic origin, and all I possess and command I place wholly and forever at the service of my own country. It is true that my nation is small, but from the very beginning it has possessed its own historical individuality. Its princes on occasions have acted in common with German princes, but the people have never regarded themselves as Germans, nor have others, during all these centuries, included them amongst them."

It, therefore, sounds very much like irony to hear Germans from the Fatherland censuring the Austrian Government for allowing the national movement among its Slavs to spread as it did. What the Austrian nations really did was to follow the advice of their Germanic tutors and awaken racially.

The population of Austria in 1910 was 28,571,934. Of this number the Slavs constituted 60.65 percentage, the Germans 35.58. It is in these figures that we must seek—and will find—the real problem of the country. "Austria," once declared a noted statesman in the Austrian Parliament, "should be a German state in language and education. German should be spoken by all persons and serve as a political bond to all races and nationalities. All the citizens, whatever may be their mother tongue, Bohemians, Slovaks, Poles, Ruthenes, Slovenes, Rumuns, and Italians, should submit to the baptism of the German school, if they desire to participate in the public affairs of the state." Someone answering von Kaiserfeld, for that was the name of the distinguished statesman, "You desire to Germanize the empire; you are not Austrians, you are Germans," von Kaiserfeld replied angrily, "There are no Austrians in Austria, only Germans." Von Kaiserfeld was not the only statesman who believed that Austria should be a German state. That is the obsession practically of every German in the country, from the emperor down to the meanest postman. Yet Austria is to-day further from the realization of this dream than it ever was. The feeling of nationalism has grown too strong among the non-Germans to be suppressed. And this nationalism demands that people shall be allowed to live their individual lives, to cultivate their language and racial ideals, and to pursue both without the interference of any other people.

Much of the difficulty in the past has been directly due to the fact that the 35 per cent. not only thought and acted for themselves, but they also insisted on doing the thinking for the 60 per cent., regardless of the latter's feelings. The result was jealousy, discord, opposition. Even the Great War which has caused Austria to rock like a rudderless ship, was engineered and premeditated by the 35 per cent., in face of the bitter, though of course futile, opposition of the 60 per cent. As a result, there is only 30 per cent. of enthusiasm and efficiency; and in juxtaposition, 60 per cent. in disaster, defeats, and discouragements.

The Hapsburgs have never learned, it seems, how to rule their many nationalities successfully. There are two races in Canada, the English and the French. If the Canadian Government had treated its citizens of French origin in the same rough-shod manner as Vienna has treated the Bohemians, or Budapest the Slovaks, Serbs, or Rumuns, she would have made rebels of every one of them, instead of loyal citizens. The Swiss Republic is the home of three races, French, German, and Italian, and yet we hear of no racial friction among them. And when and where did the national, state, or city government in the United States interfere when this or that people of foreign origin desired to build a school or establish a clubhouse?

Years ago T. G. Masaryk, a prominent Bohemian deputy, delivered a scathing denunciation in parliament, in which he took the government to task for its anti-Slavic policy. "Extirpate, Germanize, that is and has been the favorite policy of the government for decades," said Masaryk. "Extirpate whom? The Slavs, of course, and first among them the Bohemians. A nation as vigorous and virile as our Bohemian nation is bound, if persecuted, to seek and find new outlets for its surplus energy. And if, while this process is going on, we succeed in reclaiming some of the ground that had been wrested from our forefathers, it is but a law of compensation and the Germans should not claim that we are encroaching on their domain, which they claim belongs to them. We shall never rest content if we are only tolerated in Austria; we demand the right to be treated as equals with the rest of the citizens of the state and we insist on being permitted to work out our destiny as Bohemians without restrictions or limitations. We entertain no hatred toward the Germans. We are distrustful, not so much of Germany, as of Prussia. Recently a speaker in this parliament has declared that the Germans were not antagonistic to the Slavs, and that, therefore, they could not be hostile to the Bohemians. This, I regret to say, is untrue. It is a matter of common knowledge that not only they, but the government as well, are in opposition to us. I shall not repeat what Mr. Dumreicher has lately said about the Germanization of the Slovenes and of the Bohemians; permit me to allude to a pamphlet which came out some time ago and which is causing a great deal of comment, 'On the right and the duty of the Germanization of the Bohemians and the Slovenes,' by Mathias Ratkovsky. Yes, gentlemen, it will be a sin if the Bohemians and Slovenes are not Germanized, is the opinion of Mr. Ratkovsky of the Vienna Theresianum. The government should use force to attain this object, if necessary. Equality of languages, what nonsense, argues Mr. Ratkovsky! The government owes it to the people to make Bohemia German. Extirpate! Remember, gentlemen, Ratkovsky is not an isolated case; this agitation is being conducted systematically both in Austria and in Germany. F. Löher, a Bavarian historian, who studied conditions in Austria-Hungary in the seventies, declared that there was only one conclusion possible: to make Germans of Bohemians and Magyars. This same idea was advanced by Professor Walcker of the University of Leipzig. Yet, gentlemen, I should not attribute so great a weight to the opinions here cited were it not for the circumstance that bigger men in Germany were behind this scheme. One can often hear mentioned the name of Lagarde in this connection and you, gentlemen of the German national party, know Lagarde's name full well. What has this great thinker taught the German youth for decades? 'Austria must be regarded in the light of a colony of Germany. Apart from this Austria has no claim to a separate existence. Austria is confronted with one task only and that task is to Germanize all its Slavs.' To the South Slavs Lagarde gave pardon. All the other people of the Danube Monarchy, including the Magyars, were obstacles in Germany's way and the sooner they were extirpated the better for Germany, the better for themselves. Slavs, according to Lagarde, resembled a commercial enterprise which was working with an insufficient capital. And just as there could be no Reuss-Schleiz-Greiz-Lobenstein policy, so there could not exist a state called Wenzelland (an opprobrious term given to Bohemia by Germans and meaning much the same as Patrickland as applied to Ireland). Istria, contended

Lagarde, should be German to form an outlet for German commerce to the Adriatic Sea and to the African coast, Jablunkov (a town in Austrian Silesia situated on a direct route to Hungary) should hear nothing but German, and from there let the wave roll southwardly, submerging the wretched little states and people that now bar the way thither. 'No empire, save Germany, is capable of upholding peace in Central Europe, a Germany, which should reach out from the Ems to the delta of the Danube, from Memel to Trieste, from Metz to the river Bug. Only such a Germany could be self-sustaining, only such a Germany, with its huge standing army, would be powerful enough to defeat both France and Russia. Bohemians and all the other small races must not be coddled by us. On the contrary, they are our enemies, and we should deal with them as such. Austria cannot be preserved except as a Germanic Empire.' Gentlemen, note what is going on in Germany at the present time and you cannot but see that this plan to unite Austria with Germany, to Germanize Austria, has become a recognized policy in both of these monarchies. I am not quoting from newspaper clippings. I could refer you to the books of several prominent writers in support of this contention. Can you blame us then that we are on guard and that we watch with jealous look what is going on both in Germany and among our Austrian Germans? Do not tell us that we should not take seriously theories of professors lecturing at Göttingen, Münich, and so forth. No, these theories so-called are assuming practical forms. Behold, for instance, the teaching of a philosopher like Edward Hartmann. A few years ago this noted scholar defined the program of Germany very clearly: Ausrotten! (extirpate). Ausrotten whom? The Poles, of course, and with them all those who are not of German blood. You cannot convince us that this is a theory advanced by professorial dreamers only; no, it is a theory which the chancellor of iron and blood (Bismarck) put to practice with the backing and money of the Prussian Government in the case of the Poles in Posen. I allude to this not as an isolated case, but as part of a well-recognized system that is at work throughout our monarchy and that not alone threatens to undermine its very existence as a state, but which aims a death-blow at our nation, just as it menaces the life of the Poles, of the Slovenes, and of all the Slavs."

The constitution of 1867 proclaimed the equality of languages in schools, courts, and in administration of public affairs. However, the operation of this constitutional guarantee is unique and its interpretation a legal puzzle. For example, in Carinthia there are 30,000 Germans and 500,000 Slovenes; the latter are autochthons, yet the Germans there demand equality but they vehemently deny equality to the Slovene minority in Styria. In the same breath, they insist that German schools be maintained in Italian Tyrol, while they urge the authorities to close Italian schools in northern Tyrol. In Prague the courts try cases in either Bohemian or German, but should a Bohemian come into contact with the courts in Vienna, the capital of the empire, the law forgets equality and treats him there as a foreigner who must plead his case in German only. In Prague there are numerous and palatial German schools maintained by the state or the municipality, as the case may be; but in Vienna Bohemians, though numbering not less than 300,000 (in Prague Germans are 17,000 strong), have not one public school and the school authorities at the capital have fought for years in the courts every attempt of the Bohemians in that direction. A very striking illustration of the chaos in this respect is found in Bohemia. There, in the so-called German-Bohemia, Germans insist that their language shall be paramount and exclusive in the judiciary, schools, and administration. Having long enjoyed ascendency they will not content themselves with equality; yet in the rest of the country, in the mixed and in the pure Bohemian districts, they demand that both tongues shall have equal rights. By stamping their tongues as "minderwertig," inferior, the government provokes to opposition the non-German element.

Observe how the idea of equality works out in practice the matter of the distribution of schools. For 9,950,266 Germans Austria maintains 5 universities (at Vienna, Prague, Graz, Innsbruck, Czernovitz), and for 6,435,983 Bohemians one university at Prague. And this one university the Bohemians were able to get in 1882 only after a great deal of political haggling and bargaining. Opponents of the Bohemian seat of learning predicted that it would soon fail for lack of professors and of students. Yet, contrary to their expectation, when the Prague school was divided in 1882 into two parts, Bohemian and German, 1,055 students matriculated the first year in the Bohemian section as against 1,695 Germans. Eventually the Bohemian university—by the way, one of the oldest universities in Central Europe, having been founded by Emperor Charles IV. in 1348—far outstripped its old partner in point of attendance. At present the number of students in the Bohemian faculties is 4,713; in the German 2,282. Of late years a demand has been made for a second university to be located at Brno (Brünn), the capital of Moravia. The University of Prague is scandalously overcrowded and students from the sister state of Moravia are compelled, in consequence, to go to Vienna in search of education, where, under Teutonic influences, many are estranged from their nation. Numerous petitions have been addressed to the government on the subject of a second university, but to no purpose. In the matter of secondary schools (gymnasia and real schools) the discrimination against non-Germans is very striking. For 4,241,918 Bohemians in Bohemia the government maintains 39 schools of this type for secondary education, and they are unable to get more, while 2,467,724 Germans boast 34 of these schools. In Moravia the disproportion is still greater and in Silesia it is relatively worse than in Moravia. The condition of the Bohemian elementary schools in the mixed districts near the border is most deplorable. It was the blind and unreasoning hostility of the authorities in the German-Bohemian districts against Bohemian schools which led the patriots, in 1880, to found a school society called the Ústřední Matice Školská. This vernacular school society had spent, up to 1912, a total of more than $3,000,000 in the establishment and support of such schools in districts inhabited by both races. Every cent of this money has been donated by the Bohemian people in order to give their children an education in the mother tongue.

THE ORIGIN OF AUSTRIA.

"Austria as a great power," said Rieger,[18] in a speech delivered in parliament

[18] Francis L. Rieger (1818-1903), a lawyer, writer, economist, and statesman, was, despite his German name, an uncompromising patriot who had spent his whole life in the service of his nation. Modern Bohemia without Rieger is unthinkable. His name is written large on every page of his country's history. As a leader of the Old Bohemian party he naturally played a prominent rôle in the fight for the historical rehabilitation of the Bohemian

in 1861, "dates back only to the days when the Bohemian Crown and the Hungarian Crown united with Austria. We Bohemians raised it to the dignity of a state of the first magnitude when, by a free election, our diet summoned, on October 23, 1526,[19] Ferdinand I. to the sovereign throne of our kingdom. Our action was followed on November 26th of that year by the Hungarians, who placed the crown of their country on the head of this Hapsburg. From that time on Austria, composed of three states in one, started on its career of a world power. The three units were the basis, the origin, the rise of the Austrian Empire. All else is really the result of accident. Eastern Galicia has belonged to Austria only since 1772, Bukovina since 1777, Western Galicia since 1795, Venice and Dalmatia since 1797, Southern Tyrol (Trient and Brixen) since 1801, Salzburg and other smaller lands since 1814, while Cracow is part of Austria only since 1846. All these possessions have not made Austria a great power, for even without them it would still be one; however, an Austrian Empire is unthinkable and Austria as a great power is inconceivable without one of the three crowns—that of Austria, Bohemia, or Hungary."

AUSTRIA'S FUTURE DARK.

What is Austria? A land that has a German head and a Slavonic body, in which minorities rule and majorities are made to obey, the homeland of a dozen races, every one of which is dissatisfied or jealous of some other race.

There was a time when Austria had a mission to perform. That mission was to serve as the advance guard of Germandom and as a Catholic power. The first came to an end at Sedan when the Prussians assumed leadership among Germans; the second terminated when Prussia gave up its Kulturkampf against Rome. Now Austria is a country without a mission, unless it be a mission to thwart the legitimate aspirations of the Slavic races to national freedom.

For Austria to pursue further its policy of Teutonism is madness. If the monarchy wishes to live it must be neither German, for there is no room in Europe for two Germanic Empires side by side, nor wholly Slavonic, like Russia. Her manifest destiny is, or rather has been, to form a bridge between Germany and Russia, between the Slavs and Teutons, between the west and the east. For Germany to go to war to fight the Slavic peril is conceivable, even justifiable; but for Austria, more than 60 per cent. Slavonic, to draw her sword to combat Slavism sounds very much like the familiar story attributed by Plutarch to Menenius Agrippa, according to which various members of one's body determined to down the stomach as the source of all their troubles. To fight the Slavs Austria must fight herself.

Plainly the destinies of Austria and Germany are as unlike as are divergent their ambitions. Germany aspired to be a world power, a Weltmacht, and in pursuance of this dream she began to build up a colonial empire. Austria possesses no colonies. The plan of her statesmen (Aehrenthal) has been to establish a predominating Austrian influence in the Balkans, where Germany's interests, to quote the well-known words of Bismarck, were not worth the bones of one Pomeranian

Kingdom. Having married the daughter of Francis Palacký, the "Father of the Nation," he was nicknamed by his political adversaries, "Son-in-law of the Nation."

[19] Ferdinand, however, took his oath of office January 30, 1527.

grenadier. Germany is a homogeneous country or nearly so; Austria, on the contrary, is the most heterogeneous empire in Central Europe.

Quite naturally the question suggests itself: what would arise on the splendid ruins on the Danube should the proverbial ill-luck overtake the Hapsburgs in the present war? With Galicia and Bukovina lost to Russia, with Transylvania annexed to Rumania, with Trentino and Trieste restored to Italy, and Bosnia and Herzegovina incorporated in Greater Serbia—provided the partition went no further—what would be left of the Hapsburg inheritance? Instead of a Greater Austria, that should have included conquered Serbia, it is not improbable that the Hapsburgs will return home from the Great War with a Small Austria—an Austria as it began in 1527, when the Austrians, Bohemians, and Hungarians formed a confederacy and elected a Hapsburg as their ruler.

Rieger, a Bohemian statesman, once declared in the Vienna Parliament, that Austria will only live as long as the Slavs wish her to live and no longer. Rieger's famous utterance has acquired a new meaning in view of the passing events in the Hapsburg Empire.

THOMAS ČAPEK.

References: The writer of this article is largely indebted for much of the material to Professor Ernest Denis' most excellent work, *La Bohême depuis La Montagne-Blanche* (lately translated from the French into Bohemian). Among others he has consulted the following Bohemian works: *Our Re-birth, Review of Bohemian National Life Within the Last Half Century*, by Jakub Malý; *Slavdom, Pictures of Its Past and Present*. (This is a standard work containing isolated articles by a number of representative authors.) *History of Our Times*, by Dr. Jan Krištůfek; *Political History of the Bohemian Nation from the Year 1861 to the Ascension of the Badeni Ministry in 1891*, by Adolf Srb; *Political Ideas of Francis Palacký; Political Utterances and Principles of Francis L. Rieger; A Great Bohemian: The Life, Work and Meaning of Francis Palacký, the Father of the Nation*, by Václav Řezníček; *Karel Havlíček: Aims and Hopes of Political Awakening*, by T. G. Masaryk.

II.

THE SLOVAKS OF HUNGARY.

The Slovaks, a branch of the Slavic family, numbering between 2,000,000 and 3,000,000 people, and kinsmen of the Bohemians, inhabit the northwestern provinces of Hungary. There is not uniform agreement among Slovak scholars with reference to the ethnic affinity of this people with the Bohemians. Are the Slovaks a direct offshoot of the Bohemians or a separate branch of the Slavic family? Ethnologists find convincing arguments for and against both theories. Bohemians, as may be surmised, take the ground that they and the Slovaks are one—one in language and one in racial traditions—and that nothing divides them except political boundaries,—the Slovaks being subject to the rule of Hungary, Bohemians owing allegiance to Austria. Samo Czambel, a learned Slovak, published a book recently on the grammatical peculiarities of his mother tongue in which, contrary to the almost universal opinion of philologists that Slovak is but an older form of Bohemian, he contends that the old grouping of Slovak jointly with Bohemian is wrong; and that the language should be treated as an independent Slavic idiom, precisely in the same way as Polish, Russian, etc. But, though grammarians may disagree about this or that Slovak or Bohemian root or termination of a verb; though they may fancy they see a difference where probably none exists, the people themselves have no quarrels to pick, no disputes to adjust. On the contrary, they have always been good neighbors[20] and loyal friends. As for real differences of speech, these are so slight that a Slovak will understand a Bohemian as readily as an Englishman from Yorkshire will his cousin, the Yankee. One is reminded of the closeness of the two languages when one recalls that Slovaks of the Protestant faith read at their church services from the Bohemian Bible. Recently a meeting of representative Bohemians and Slovaks[21] in New York passed a resolution, in which occurs this significant passage: "Nothing now separates us, except that we owe political allegiance to two different states, one to Austria, the other to Hungary. Remove that barrier, and it will be seen that the Bohemians and Slovaks are one in language, one in blood, one in national faith, indissoluble and indivisible."

According to the census of 1910, a census, by the way, notoriously unreliable, Slovaks number 1,967,970. If an enumeration were taken free of intrigue and coercion, the actual number of Slovaks, it is asserted, would be nearer 2,500,000;

[20] "The Slovaks and Their Language" (Slováci a ich Reč), by Dr. Samo Czambel, Budapest, 1903.

[21] Among the Slovak spokesmen at this meeting was Editor Milan Getting, of New York. At a subsequent conference was present Albert Mamatey, President of the National Slovak Society.

and, were we to include as Slovaks the opportunists who everywhere go with the ruling element, and further, were we to add those who are compelled, for various reasons, to conceal their nationality, the actual number would not be far from 3,000,000. Outside of Slovakland Slovaks are scattered throughout Hungary except in Transylvania. There are few districts in Hungary in which they do not live. The various settlements in the interior of the country are in part ramifications of Slovakland proper, which formerly extended further south into Hungary than at present and in part colonies, the origin of which dates back to the eighteenth and nineteenth centuries.

When did the Slovaks come to Hungary? Probably the question could best be answered by saying that they had always lived there. Certain pseudo-historians wish to make it appear that the Slovaks are descendants of immigrants from Bohemia who fled to Hungary to escape religious and political persecution. The truth is, however, that their ancestors occupied the Carpathian highlands from the dawn of history. The Slovaks of Hungary are not immigrants, and no authoritative historian has successfully disputed their claim to priority as one of the earliest inhabitants of the Kingdom of St. Stephen.

Down to the middle of the last century no one of the languages spoken by the different racial elements in Hungary acquired predominance. For the purposes of every-day life each race was free to use its mother tongue. During the mediæval period Latin was the medium of communication among the cultured classes. Latin was gradually superseded by the German language and the Slovaks, though grieved at the wanton suppression of their vernacular, did not feel that their national existence had been threatened by the innovation. But when, in 1867, Austria concluded with Hungary the Act of Settlement, whereby the dual system of government was introduced, and the Magyars secured for themselves ascendency over all the other races in the kingdom, the danger became acute, and has been growing steadily since, until now the Slovaks are menaced by denationalization. True, the Law of Nationalities was promulgated soon after the Act of Settlement, ostensibly for the protection of non-Magyars; but this law, in the words of Plutarch, "is like a spider web and would catch the weak and the poor; but may easily be broken by the mighty rich." Bitter experience has shown that under the Law of Nationalities, the very acts which the law was designed to prevent or regulate, have been perpetrated with impunity, either by omission or commission.

Students of Slovak nationality have been expelled by school authorities from seminaries and secondary schools for Pan-Slavic propaganda. Pan-Slavism in the case of these unfortunate youths consists in the reading, recitation, or circulation of literature in one of the Slavic tongues.

Journalists are prosecuted or jailed for alleged seditious articles against the Hungarian State; newspapers are mulcted in ruinous fines, in many cases tantamount to their suppression. In countries enjoying the blessing of freedom of speech and press, *de facto* and not only *de jure*, the articles which Hungarian prosecuting attorneys construe as seditious, would be regarded as an honest and fearless criticism of the acts of government. There are few Slovak journalists who have not served terms in jail or whose newspapers have not been fined.

To plead one's case in the courts in the Slovak language, notwithstanding the express provisions of the Law of Nationalities permitting this procedure, would be prejudicial to the litigant's case in the lower courts and impossible in the higher courts.

A patriotic Slovak may not hold a government position of any trust or importance. One aspiring to an office in any way connected with the government, directly or indirectly, must of necessity renounce his nationality—or, in the alternative, conceal his true inward feelings, both before his superiors and before his friends.

Apparently with the object of making the world believe that Slovakland has always been Magyar, the Hungarian Government is abolishing the ancient Slavic nomenclature of villages and towns, replacing it with Magyar names, and this crusade is undertaken in districts where from times immemorial no other speech had been heard but Slovak.[22]

A visiting Hungarian statesman boasted before an American audience in New York City that the laws of Hungary were as broad and liberal as those in the United States. If such were the case, why are not Slovaks permitted to establish schools and organize themselves into societies as freely as in the United States? In the early seventies of the last century the government closed all the Slovak secondary schools (gymnasia) on the pretext that they fostered among the pupils and professors Pan-Slavic propaganda. Since that time, and despite the plain language of the Law of Nationalities, assuring to every race education in its native tongue, Slovaks have been unable to obtain from the authorities consent to the reopening of even one higher school. Think of a nation of two millions and a half, living in the heart of Europe, not having one higher school for the education of its youth! In 1875 the government confiscated the funds of an educational institution, and with the money undertook to publish at Budapest "a patriotic Hungarian journal." At the University of Budapest, the Slovak idiom is studiously ignored by the instructors, though the Slovaks are heavy taxpayers, and even a biased census concedes 10 per cent. Slovak population in the country. Slovak elementary schools are fast disappearing; those that still remain in Slovakland are either mixed, that is Slovak-Magyar, or pure Magyar. Under the provision of the Apponyi Law, Magyar is the only recognized language of instruction in elementary schools in Hungary which are attended by twenty or more Magyar children. Since the normal schools are all Magyar, it is obvious that the future teachers of Slovak children will have no means, except by private study, to learn the language of their little charges.

Neither Vienna nor Budapest will listen to their appeal for justice. The Lord is too high and the Emperor-King too far away to hear and see the Slovaks. The Rumuns in Transylvania may hope for succor from their motherland, Rumania; Italians in the unredeemed provinces may look forward to the time when Italy will liberate them from Austrian misrule; even the Serbs in Southern Hungary find new courage in resisting oppression by reason of their nearness to their brothers in the Serbian Kingdom. Whence shall Slovaks look for sympathy and help? Their

---

[22] The very words "Slovak," "Slovakland," "Slovak nation" are tabooed in Hungary, and school books containing them prohibited. Hungarian officialdom refers to Slovakland as the Hungarian Highlands.

nearest kinsmen, the Bohemians, who, of all the nations, best understand them, are themselves held down by an alien oppressor and unable to give them other than moral aid.

"In comparison with the Government of Magyarland the Government of Austria is a model of tolerance."[23]

This is the opinion of an Englishman who knows conditions in Hungary well. Exterminate the race, suppress its language, obliterate every evidence of its existence: that is now and has been for decades the policy of the Hungarian Government toward the Slovaks.

Some time ago the American Slovaks formulated a demand for autonomy in a memorandum which they sent to influential friends and to those whom they hope to win as friends. The memorandum "voices the sentiment and national aspirations, not only of Slovaks living in the United States, but also interprets the mind and the will of their brothers, inhabiting, since times immemorial, the ancestral homelands of the race." That the American Slovaks took the initiative in issuing the memorandum is not hard to understand. "The Slovaks at home are not permitted to approach their king with grievances, the last deputation to him having been denied admittance. Slovaks, therefore, are made to feel that they have no king, only a government—a government, however, that knows no mercy, that feels no remorse, that offers no hope, that fears no punishment. If Slovaks are resolved to speak at all, if they wish the world at large to know the measure of their wrongs, under existing conditions, they can only appeal through the medium of their compatriots in the United States."

Of the Magyars as a nation the Slovaks do not complain. It is the Hungarian Government which they accuse of oppression.

When the time approaches to re-draw the map of Austria-Hungary, the Slovaks will ask to be freed from the Hungarian yoke. And if they cannot have a government of their own, their second choice is to co-operate with the Bohemians toward the establishment of a confederacy that shall include the autonomous states of Bohemia, Moravia, Silesia, and Slovakland. Thus to the present ethnical unity of Slovaks and Bohemians another bond would be added, that of political unity.

THOMAS ČAPEK.

References: *The Slovaks of Hungary*, The Knickerbocker Press, New York, 1906, by Thomas Čapek; *Racial Problems in Hungary*, Archibald Constable & Co., Ltd., London, 1908, by Scotus Viator. *Die Unterdrückung der Slovaken durch die Magyaren*, Prague, 1903.

---

[23] London *Times*, January 20, 1915.

III.

WHY BOHEMIA DESERVES FREEDOM.

By Professor B. Šimek of the State University of Iowa[24]

In the present European crisis several nations are hoping for a betterment of their political fortunes. Among these not the least hopeful are the Bohemians in the historic Kingdom of Bohemia, now annexed to the Austrian Empire.

Many who are unfamiliar with the situation will probably ask: Why should the Bohemians seek independence? Are they not more secure as a part of a large empire? It is in anticipation of, and in response to such questions that the following facts are presented.

Bohemia has not received just treatment at the hands of the Austrian Government. Her national spirit has been offended or ignored, her people have been oppressed, her schools are not adequately maintained, and the scant support which they now receive has been wrung from the government only by tremendous effort, and in times of great political stress. Even now the people are compelled to maintain schools in some parts of the kingdom by voluntary contributions. The government has done nothing for Bohemia either politically, intellectually, or industrially, excepting under compulsion. Therefore there is no reason for a grateful desire to perpetuate the present relation. Bohemia has heretofore been loyal to Austria only because she faced a greater danger from German absorption.

The grounds on which the Bohemians ask the right to shape their own destinies as a nation are chiefly the following:

1. The historic right.—The House of Hapsburg was called to the throne of Bohemia by voluntary election. The first Hapsburg to attempt to rule Bohemia was Rudolph (1306-1307), who was forced upon the country for a short time by the German Emperor, and who attempted to secure the color of a right to rule by marrying the widow of the last Bohemian King of the Přemysl line. His right to rule was contested, and upon his death the Bohemians selected several kings from other ruling houses, and it was not until 1437 that another Hapsburg, Albrecht, was again voluntarily elected King of Bohemia. But after a brief rule of two years, during which he violated his oath and his pledges to the Bohemian people, he was again succeeded by a line of kings elected from various ruling houses, and the greatest of them, George of Poděbrad, the Protestant king who ruled from 1458 to

[24] The writer is a representative type of the sturdy settler of Bohemian ancestry who helped to build up the Northwest. He sojourned in the birthland of his parents when the war broke out.

1471, from among their own nobility.

It was not until 1526 that another Hapsburg, Ferdinand I., was elected king by the Bohemian Diet, but he soon destroyed the old charter in accordance with which he was recognized as a king by election, and usurped the power which the House of Hapsburg continued to exercise for some time. But in 1619 the Bohemians reasserted their right to elect their kings and chose Frederick of the Palatinate, thus precipitating the Thirty Years' War. But notwithstanding the reverses which the Bohemians suffered, Ferdinand II. of Hapsburg, who ascended the throne, was obliged to take oath "to maintain the privileges and liberties of the kingdom" and to "govern the kingdom according to the laws and usages of the kings, his predecessors, and especially Charles IV."

During the long dark night which followed the deep tragedy of the Thirty Years' War, the Hapsburgs ruled over Bohemia, but the nation never conceded them the right to incorporate their country in any other, and in 1868 formally declared that "the Kingdom of Bohemia is attached to the empire by a purely personal tie,"—that is, through the person of the king who was also Emperor of Austria. Francis Josef himself soon after recognized this right and promised to be crowned King of Bohemia, but this promise was broken.

For the reasons here given the Bohemians claim that their kingdom is still a distinct political entity.

2. Their political capacity.—Time and again the Bohemians have demonstrated their loyalty to high political ideals and their capacity for self-government. They never recognized the "divine right" of kings to rule,—unlike their German neighbors, most of whom recognize the "right" to-day. They elected their own kings, who were bound by what was practically equivalent to our modern constitution, and they sometimes chose these kings from their own midst; before the outbreak of the Thirty Years' War they were seriously contemplating a form of government not unlike that of our own country; and to-day they are hoping for a republic, or at least for a monarchy as liberal and innocuous as that of England. Indeed, for several centuries their political ideals have approached nearer to those of England than of any other of the greater European nations.

3. Their intellectual power.—A nation claiming the right of self-government is usually expected to show competent intellectual capacity. This the Bohemians have demonstrated beyond a doubt. When we consider the great odds against which they contended when they struggled to re-establish their schools and their intellectual life, the progress which they have made in the past century is astonishing. The city of Prague is to-day one of the greatest publishing centres in Europe. The growth of Bohemian literature in all its branches has been stupendous, and to-day Bohemia leads the Empire of Austria with the smallest percentage of illiterates and is one of the leaders of Europe in this respect!

Nor are these educational and intellectual ideals a gift of the Germans, as has been asserted in certain prejudiced quarters. Bohemia had a great university, that of Prague, before a single institution of the kind had been established within the limits either of the present German Empire or any other part of the present Empire of Austria. This has been claimed repeatedly as a German university, but it was established in 1348 by Charles IV., whose mother was a Bohemian, and whose sentiments were wholly Bohemian. He was educated in the University of Paris, and that institution furnished the model for his new university. Following the Paris plan he gave two votes to the German nations in the management of the university (a courtesy which they have never been inclined to imitate), but like all other institutions of that period the university was Latin, and not in any sense German. Fifty years later it passed wholly under the control of the Bohemians and developed into one of the greatest universities of Europe, sharing this honor with Paris and Oxford, and for more than two centuries it continued to be one of the world's great centres of intellectual activity and inspiration. The Thirty Years' War overwhelmed it, and transformed it into a German institution for a long time, but a third of a century ago it was re-established as a Bohemian institution, and has now far outstripped its German rival in the same city which was forced upon the nation in the effort to Germanize it.

It is also a matter of historic interest that as early as 1294 a King of Bohemia, Václav II., attempted to establish a university at Prague, but the plan failed because of dissensions between the ecclesiastics and the nobility.

The Bohemian people have abundant intellectual traditions of their own, and their devotion to their educational interests has been tested repeatedly and found not wanting.

4. The moral and ethical right.—Why should any other nation rule Bohemia? The Bohemian people are intellectual, with high political ideals and splendid traditions, and they are industrially progressive. They are competent to direct their own affairs, and it is only the insolent usurper who can assume to lay claim to the right to rule over them. Bohemia is a fertile country blessed with boundless riches which should be employed to sustain a happy, busy, progressive nation, and not a usurping military power, and that nation has a right to be free!

This briefly is the Bill of Rights of the Bohemian nation. Whatsoever may be the form of the government which will come to liberated Bohemia, all lovers of freedom will join in the hope of the realization of the spirit of the prophecy of Doctor John Jesenský of Jesen, one of the martyr leaders of the Bohemians who were executed at Prague in 1621, who proclaimed from the scaffold: "It is vain that Ferdinand gluts his rage for blood; a king elected by us shall again ascend the throne of Bohemia!"

PROFESSOR BOHUMIL ŠIMEK.

IV.

THE BOHEMIAN CHARACTER.

By Herbert Adolphus Miller, Ph.D., Professor of Sociology,
Oberlin College, Ohio[25]

The mental and moral characteristics of any social group are the product of a wide variety of complex influences of a pre-eminently psychological nature. The suggestions that come through tradition and history result in mental reactions that become so typical of the group that it is popular to call them inborn and racial. The easy assumption of this explanation hinders the more fundamental discovery of why certain characteristics prevail. The Bohemians illustrate this principle of the creative influence of definite ideas.

A Bohemian is a Slav. The influence of this relationship is the broadest and most general. It has become self-conscious only in comparatively recent times, i.e., two or three generations. Previously there was much changing from Slav to Teuton and vice versa. Unquestionably a very large proportion of Prussians have a considerable infusion of Slavic blood, and many Bohemians have German ancestors. In centres like Pilsen or Prague, where the two races have lived together for a long time, it is absolutely impossible to tell them apart until they begin to speak, and then the identity may be concealed by using the other language. Within the last seventy-five years there has been a clear recognition of the Slavic relationship which has taken the form of conscious efforts to preserve certain Slavic characteristics, and to join with the others in withstanding the influence and authority of the Germans. There have been certain other Slavic characteristics that have persisted in all the Slavic groups which will be mentioned later when we consider their contribution to democracy.

For something over five hundred years the Bohemians have been clearly conscious of their Bohemian nationality and much that is distinctive of them has been developed and is still being developed in them by this national history, and nothing of it can be understood except in the light of this historical influence. The two most influential forces have been John Hus, who made Bohemia Protestant a century before Luther, and who was burned at the stake in 1415; and Comenius the world educator, who was exiled for his connection with the Protestant Church of Bohemian Brethren. These two national heroes planted the seeds which differentiated the Bohemians from the rest of the Slavs in religious freedom and respect for

---

[25] Professor Miller has traveled in Bohemia and is gathering material on the history of that country.

education. Hus also was the symbol for the development of nationalism and the consequent revival of the language which have occupied such a large place in the attention of the Bohemian people. The two most characteristic expressions of these influences are now found in Nationalism and Free-thought, and no appreciation of the condition and purposes of the people can be complete without reckoning with these facts.

From about 1400 for more than two hundred years Bohemia was a leader in European culture, but the Thirty Years' War crushed her so that some claim that she has had no history since 1620. Count Lützow says that "Bohemia presents the nearly unique case of a country which was formerly almost entirely Protestant and has become almost entirely Catholic. The popular optimistic fallacy which maintains that in no country has the religious belief been entirely suppressed by persecution and brute force is disproved by the fate of Bohemia." As a matter of fact, instead of being suppressed, it was smouldering during the centuries and now constitutes an amazing unanimity of mind and feeling among the nation in regard to religion. Immediately after the Act of Tolerance in 1781 there sprang up here and there churches which took up the old faith exactly where it had been left more than a hundred and fifty years before. Free-thinking is in part a philosophy, but it is more particularly a sign of national character.

In the past it has been the custom of nations to try to absorb all within their political boundaries into the character of the governing group, however much they may have differed in traditions and customs. Austria not only tried to make Bohemians Catholics but Germans, and the history of the effort ought to make clear for ever that political science must adjust itself to the laws of human nature, and that the way to develop the individualism of a people is to try to blot it out. Whatever may be said about the superiority of one culture over another it cannot be imposed by force, and the Germans have been stupidly slow in discovering this fundamental fact. Bohemia is but a single example of this new consciousness which is called Nationalism. The Poles, Lithuanians, Finns, Magyars, Irish, and all the Slavic groups are showing that there is a psychological force to be reckoned with which military force cannot overcome. The contribution of the variety of cultures is what will enrich the life of civilization and not the pre-eminence of one, whatever that one may be. Some evidence of the way in which the revival of nation spirit is taking place among the Bohemians will show what a tremendous force this spirit is.

Count Lützow, in an address given in Prague in 1911, brings out the present situation: "One of the most interesting facts that in Bohemia and especially in Prague mark the period of peace at the beginning of the nineteenth century is the revival of the national feeling and language.... The greatest part of Bohemia, formerly almost Germanized, has now again become thoroughly Slavic. The national language, for a time used only by the peasantry in outlying districts, is now freely and generally used by the educated classes in most parts of the country. Prague itself, that had for a time acquired almost the appearance of a German town, has now a thoroughly Slavic character. The national literature also, which had almost ceased to exist, is in a very flourishing state, particularly since the foundation of a national university. At no period have so many and so valuable books been written in the Bohemian language."

About sixty years ago several Bohemian writers were bold enough to write in their own language instead of German and from that time the Bohemian spirit has grown until opposition to the overbearing Germanism became almost a passion. Wherever the Germans were in a majority only German public schools were provided, but wherever the municipality had fewer Germans than Slavs German as well as Bohemian schools were provided. To meet this discrimination Bohemians, both at home and in America, have contributed to a remarkable degree for the "Mother of Schools" (association) which supports Bohemian schools of first caliber in the minority communities. There are no other Slavs who compare with the Bohemians in the high regard for schools. As one goes through the country he is struck by the palatial school building even in poor peasant villages. It seems to bear a relation similar to the prison and church in a Russian town. The inevitable result of this universal spirit is the gradual elimination of the German language. German had nearly vanished from the streets of Prague. One fared ill in a restaurant if his German were good enough to sound genuine though the waiter understood perfectly. Business men were beginning to take pride in the fact that they could succeed without knowing any German, and fathers who were reared with German as a mother tongue taught their children Bohemian instead. The unifying force of this national feeling has been going on with great rapidity in the face of the disrupting force of eleven political parties, besides the sharp spiritual division into Catholics and anti-Catholics.

It could not fail to be a distinct disadvantage for a people of seven or eight million to cut itself off from the opportunities of the environing German culture, science, and commerce, but those who saw this most clearly deliberately assumed the cost in their struggle for the freedom of the spirit. When we remember that prestige was on the side of the German one sees a sacrifice approaching nobility. At the time the Olympic games were being held in Europe and attracting the attention of the world a far more important athletic meet was being held in Prague. This was Slavic in its membership, though Bohemian in its origin. More than twenty thousand persons took part, and at one time eleven thousand men, speaking several different languages, were doing calisthenic exercises together. With the exception of the Poles, who would not come because the Russians were invited, there were representatives of all the Slavic nationalities, and the keynote of every speech was "Slavie! Slavie!" and when it was uttered the crowds would go wild. There were a quarter of a million visitors in the city, and illustrated reports of the exhibition went to the ends of the Slavic world. A few weeks afterwards I saw some of them pasted on the wall of a primitive factory in the back districts of Moscow. But the German papers completely ignored the whole thing and no self-respecting German could attend, though it was undoubtedly the greatest thing of the sort ever held.

Two years ago when war was threatening between Austria and Serbia, Bohemians who were being entrained from their garrison for mobilization on the Serbian border, in more than one case sang the Pan-Slavic hymn, "Hej Slované!"

familiar to all Slavic nations, but forbidden to Austrian soldiers in service. They used a popular parody in this enthusiastic and powerful hymn, full of encouragement to the Slavs, telling them that their language shall never perish nor shall they "even though the number of Germans equal the number of souls in hell." It is said that at this time at least seventy thousand Slavs in Austria eligible to military service quit the country.

The Germans have succeeded in making the Bohemian culture almost identical with theirs, and it is difficult to find in the German any traits that can be called specifically Bohemian. Only a long future can tell whether there are actually inherent psychological differences which can account for aggressiveness in the one and passivity in the other. We may assume, however, that we have not had time to test the subtle forces which work on social groups and give them a cast of thought that seems biologically inherent. No Slavic people has exhibited the individualistic character of the Teuton, but we have no assurance that this Teuton habit of mind is the result of anything except the history and the philosophy which have been appropriated in comparatively modern times. There are two ways of explaining the relative passivity of the Slavic mind. One is the fact that having been for so long a subject people they have no traditions of success. Even the Russians are ruled by a bureaucracy with which they have no sympathy. The other is that the Bohemians and the others have retained the democratic characteristics which are common to the Slavs. There has been some influence from both.

One peculiarity of Bohemians both in America and Bohemia is the habit of criticising any of their own people who acquire any eminence or leadership in any field. One never feels free to speak with enthusiasm about a successful Bohemian lest he invite a dash of cold water. There seems to be universal suspicion of the motives or methods underlying the success. If a leader were to appear he would not get followers. Such a habit of mind can never bring anything that corresponds to imperialistic success. Count Lützow says "that the evil seed of hatred and distrust sown by the oppressors in the seventeenth and eighteenth centuries bears evil fruit up to the present day. Bohemian peasants even now instinctively distrust the nobles of their own race who are in full sympathy with the national cause. This antagonism has frequently contributed to the failure of the attempts of the Bohemians to recover their autonomy."

There is a great difference in an individual or a people that has been accustomed to accomplishment. The attitude in Bohemia has been that of pessimistic resignation. Their devotion to certain ideals and causes is magnificent, but the inability to organize unanimously is indicated by the eleven political parties, most of which are nationalistic and none of which has the active co-operation of the masses. They follow an ideal rather than a person, and the symbol of the ideal is always a person who is dead. The look is thus backward rather than hopefully forward. Hus is the great hero, but also Comenius, Palacký, Havlíček, and many others of more or less remoteness are the real leaders, and the reinstatement of national self-direction and the Bohemian language are the ideal objects.

In Bohemia these result in an impracticalness which magnifies the æsthetic even to sentimentality. They will talk as though art were the end of life. For many the æsthetic life consists of sitting in restaurants night after night listening to the band and talking over their beer. In spite of this industry has made great progress in Bohemia, and when they come to this country they forget their objection to the practical. There are probably no other immigrants in America who make such direct efforts to own their own homes as the Bohemians. At a gathering of instructors of the University of Prague to organize a sociological institute, I was asked to tell some of the things we do here. I tried to show how we combine theory with practice and emphasized my own interest which is theoretical, but they unanimously said that our methods were too practical to be used by them.

A comparison of Poles and Bohemians who belong to the same race shows the influence of culture on the Bohemian. In 1900 the percentage of illiterates among the Bohemians entering the United States was 3. and of Poles 31.6. The Poles are as strongly the Catholic as the Bohemians are Free-thinkers.

In Austria there are fourteen times as many cases of litigation in the courts among the Poles as among the Bohemians. A Bohemian in Chicago who does a large mail order business among all Slavs says: "We will not do business with the Poles at all because they will not pay. To the Serbians we send everything C.O.D., but the Croatians, Ruthenians, and the rest we trust."

The family life is an important sign of the morality of a people, and we find among the Bohemians many interesting qualities. The following statement in "Hull House Papers" derived from a study of Bohemians says: "The family life is affectionate, and it is the prevailing custom among the working class to give all the wages to the mother." I have often noticed that in families the income is naturally estimated as the total earnings of husband and children and that the mother gives even to the larger children who are earning good wages what money they need, and always with cheerfulness and perfect understanding. The attachment for the home is very strong, and they take pride in large families which stick together. It is probable that ownership of the home works both ways in this matter, having the home integrates the family and having the family unity makes it desirable to own a home.

In sex morality we must remember that the Bohemians are European and not American, but on the streets of Prague there is less public display of immorality than in Chicago. Modesty is observed as an important virtue. The Bohemians, like all other people, have prejudices that make it difficult for them to see clearly values not measured by their own standard, but there can be no question but that their standard measures up well with any people in Europe. The important thing to civilization is whether they have any peculiar traits of mind or character that will be a contribution to progress. I think that the Bohemians have this in common with the other Slavs to a very marked degree and in a direction which has hitherto been entirely unrecognized, and this is the contribution to democracy.

However else the Germans may justify the present war, they sincerely believe that on their success hangs the salvation of civilization from the barbarism of the half-civilized Slav. Professors Eucken and Haeckel have voiced a widespread indignation that England could so far forget her ideals as to join with Russia against the forces of enlightenment. Americans, even those whose sympathies are hostile to Germans, dread success of the Russians. The socialists who are opposed to all war feel convinced that Russia is a menace to all their plans. In fact they have tacitly admitted more than once that it might be necessary to resist encroachments of Russia by force. It is my contention that the Slavic people, of whom the Russians are the largest group, have more to contribute to what the world needs next than any other people, and that all that is best in socialism will find its fruition among them as nowhere else.

A learned Bohemian friend, in reply to my letter to Bohemia, in which I spoke of the political progress America was making, said that it could but fill the heart of a Bohemian "with a feeling of sad resignation"; but he adds, "I am not pessimistic enough to give up all hope that Providence may have yet some good things in store for the Slav. What keeps me up is a certain hazy impression that human development may sometime be in want of a new formula, and then our time may come. I conceive ourselves under the sway of the German watchword which spells Force; and as watchwords, like everything else human, come and go, perhaps the Slavs may sometime be called on to introduce another, which I should like to see spelled Charity."

There is no literature in the world which has contributed so much toward such a sentiment as that of the Slavs. Tolstoy is the great example, and his very greatness enabled him to propose a program even beyond present imagination, but many other writers, some of whom have been translated and some not, have expressed the same ideal of needed radical reform. We must not make the mistake of thinking these writers the originators of their doctrines. A popular prophet expresses the heart of the people, and is a product of their ideals. The great vogue of these writers is among their own people. The government of Russia is hostile to Tolstoy, but it could not resist the demands of the students that an heroic statue of this radical be placed in the great government technical school.

The ultimate goal of society is democracy and, strange as it may sound, the Slav has more to contribute to this end than anyone else. Russia, whose name is the synonym of despotism, is already in reality the most democratic country in the world. Democracy means the opportunity for the individual to express himself to the utmost, to have his expression count according to its value, and if he does not predominate to yield gracefully to the expression that does prevail. This habit of mind cannot be obtained without practice, and up to the present time in the world's history would not have been as efficient as the leadership of individuals who, right or wrong, obtained results. Now by means of rapid communication and a clearer understanding of social purposes the method of democracy can be applied with increasing efficiency. Nurture in democratic practice is the contribution the Slavs will make, and we cannot realize how rich this will be.

The despotism of Russia is no more an expression of the real Russian people than Tammany Hall is an expression of American democracy, and the influence of both institutions on national character has been practically nothing. Despotisms come and go, but the traditions and customs of the people persist. It was formerly thought that ideals were imposed from above, but now we are becoming pretty thoroughly convinced that this is not the case. Imitation is horizontal between people of the same class and not vertical between classes. Polish nobles had glass windows for years, but it did not occur to the peasants to have them until the idea was brought back from America by people of their own sort. And so influences and habits may go on for centuries upon centuries without being affected by a different culture. This fortunate fact has enabled us to preserve what would have been eliminated by the contemporary values and customs that were not valuable for the time.

Any observant traveler entering Russia, after he gets over the first fear which everyone seems to feel, will gradually be impressed with the contrast to the Germans and Austrians whom he has just left. There he was never addressed without his full title of Herr Professor, Herr Journalist, or whatever he might claim for his distinction. Here his self-esteem suffers a shock, for, in the language of the country, he becomes simply "Mister." This universal custom, unimportant in itself, is significant of a national habit of mind. Men in high places, as heads of universities, are addressed by their colleagues by their first names. In the familiar Russian and Polish novel we find nobles and military leaders regularly with the simple title Pan (Mr.), which is a term of respect but not of distinction. In fact the attitude of the noble and the peasant toward each other is not that of superiority and servility, but as elder and younger brother. The name Little Father which is applied to the Czar expresses the attitude of familiarity rather than of awe. Compare this with the worship of uniform in Germany, where a policeman will not answer your question unless you salute him and an omitted title is an insult. In Petrograd during student riots it is not an uncommon thing for the students to kick the shins of the police and no one thinks of it as lèse majesté. The Russian officer and soldier are more nearly comrades than in any other army in the world.

These habits have not been assumed deliberately, but are the product of underlying institutions out of which they have grown naturally. At least fifty million people in Greater Russia and Siberia live in Mirs or Communes. In these from time immemorial they have practiced a degree of co-operation and local self-government which has never been equalled by deliberate action in the most enlightened nations, and which the most despotic government, not being able to overthrow, has recently incorporated into its governmental method. In the Mir the land which is owned in common is regularly reallotted among the householders according to their working capacities and needs. The Mir elects its own executive and may undertake all kinds of work of public utility. Occasionally a woman is elected as executive, and when the man representing the household is away or dead the woman votes and takes part in the assembly. The Mirs are united into larger bodies with similar jurisdiction. The interesting thing about it is that it prevails so widely and among people between whom there has not been the slightest possibility of intercommunication. The promise of the Mir is not communism, but a habit of mind that can be applied in more general and complex affairs.

Complaint has more or less justly been made that the Slav is deficient in political leadership except in the smallest units. This can have been true in the past while holding for a future under quite different conditions. Ease of communication has enlarged social units so that common ideas may result in common action over wide areas as easily as in a common room. At any rate the Slavs have succeeded in carrying over their custom in a very remarkable manner. The *artel*, which is a co-operative productive organization, embraces most diverse enterprises throughout Russia, and is efficient in a manner only dreamed of elsewhere. Tiffany's finest silver enamel is mostly made by peasant *artels* in Moscow. In one small factory where most of the men were away getting in their harvests, the rest were making beautiful inlaid Easter eggs, and a special order of ice cream dishes worth a hundred dollars apiece, yet these work-owners were so untouched by modern customs and the civilization for which they were producing that they ate their dinner from a common dish with wooden spoons. The porters at the railroad stations are *artels* governed by their own rules and sharing the proceeds. Many banks and large enterprises are carried on in the same way. One of the largest restaurants in Petrograd is owned by the men who do the work. Fishing is also co-operative in its methods. Undertakings of this sort could not possibly be carried through so generally and so successfully if it were not for the great background of experience in which co-operation and acquiescence to the will of the people is accepted as a matter of course.

We recognize that one of the greatest problems of our time is that of class consciousness between labor and capital, and economists have suggested co-operation as the only cure for the deadlock that threatens, but it has not succeeded where tried. The Russians have succeeded without being conscious that they were doing any but the most natural thing. For people who have been forbidden so much that is thought to be essential to freedom, it is nothing short of remarkable, that in the recent years of industrial progress and increasing complexity, they should have been able to adapt their democracy to fit the needs. Nowhere are labor unions formed more easily, and while meager in their activities, as compared to American or English, they have coherence.

The church has developed in line with the characteristics of the people. Although the Orthodox Church is magnificent in its equipment, and its priests most richly caparisoned, yet it offers a marked contrast to the aristocratic system of the Roman Catholic Church. The Russian most devoutly takes off his hat in passing a church or holy image, but he keeps it on when passing the priest, and he kisses the priest on the cheek rather than the hand.

Among other Slavs there is the same widespread prevalence of democratic customs. In Serbia the Mir is found in much the same form as in Russia, and in Poland in numerous instances the Zadruga is a community of from ten to sixty or more living in one house and settling important matters by vote. The head of the Zadruga is generally the oldest man, but this is not necessary, and not infrequently a woman is head. In the days of its independence the Polish king was always elected. The suffrage was restricted to the nobles, and much turbulence prevailed at the time of election, but the people were very jealous of the privilege.

Of all the Slavs the Bohemians have come most under German influence and it has often been said that the assimilation is all in the direction of the German. In many characteristics this is true, but some of the traditional habits of mind have clearly been preserved. They have not lost these by being transferred to America and are able to carry on certain forms of association with phenomenal success. In Chicago they have 104 Building and Loan Associations incorporated under the laws of Illinois. All are prosperous, only one has ever failed. Each has only one paid officer, a secretary who receives from five to ten dollars a week. One association has assets of $600,000, and all of them aggregate about $14,000,000 and 20,000 members. They also have numerous benevolent lodges with an aggregate membership of over 100,000 in the United States, which manage insurance systems on a most democratic and safe basis. This management in almost all cases includes women in exact equality. The same thing is true of the Sokol or gymnastic society which is organized in all Slavic countries. In the numerous deliberative meetings of Bohemians that I have attended the women have shown themselves quite the equal of the men in debate.

The ultimate democracy must include universal suffrage, which we see has its roots in the Slavic institutions. The Bohemians have the arguments of the Germans about the place of women, but their practice is more subtly democratic than they are aware of. Until it was confused with the prohibition question Bohemians have consistently advocated equal suffrage, before it became generally popular. The Germans have as consistently opposed it.

Whatever the outcome of the war the Slavs will inevitably become an increasing influence in the world's progress because of their higher birth rate and because they possess the richest natural resources in the world. It is perhaps an occasion for gratitude that in the midst of the apparently insoluble problems about the exploitation of natural resources and labor conflicts, a people that has been nurturing in what we have called barbarism the traits most desirable for dealing with such problems, is now about to come upon the stage.

To be sure, most of the Slavic world is permeated by ignorance and dominated by bureaucracy, but education is only a generation deep, and political reorganization is the most rapid and remarkable fact of our era. The Bohemians have shown us that under modern conditions these traits are not lost. Civilization may have a temporary setback, but it cannot be as great as that now arising from militarism, but in the end the Slav will contribute to the social fabric that for which it is now peculiarly ready. In the words of an ancient writer we may say that the stone which the builder rejected is become the head of the corner.

Professor H. A. Miller.

V.

PLACE OF BOHEMIA IN THE CREATIVE ARTS.

By Will S. Monroe, Professor State Normal School, Montclair, N. J.,
Author of "Bohemia and the Čechs,"
"Comenius and the Beginnings of Educational Reform," etc.[26]

It remains to call attention to the place of Bohemia in letters, art, music, education, social and religious reform. In this connection it may be pointed out that the civilization of the Bohemians is distinctly older than that of the German-Austrians, and that it developed wholly independent of the Teutonic art movements in Germany and Austria.

In the matter of literature, Bohemia occupies a place of distinction and priority. The development of the vulgar tongue took place at a comparatively early period. Some of the most ancient of the poetic documents date back to very early times. Indeed, the prose literature of Bohemia, after the Greek and Latin, is one of the oldest in Europe. The three centuries from the time of Charles IV. to the outbreak of the Thirty Years' War covers the early brilliant period in literature. Two centuries of intellectual barrenness followed the fatal battle of the White Mountain and the usurpation of the Bohemian Crown by the House of Hapsburg. The ancient constitution of the kingdom was suppressed and it was replaced by a slightly veiled system of Teutonic absolutism. The lands of the Bohemian nobles, who had been patrons of letters, were confiscated and given to generals in the Austrian army and to Austrian noblemen. The inhabitants of the flourishing cities, that had been strongholds of the national language and literature, were driven into exile and their places were taken by immigrants of non-Bohemian birth. The country people were reduced to a state of serfdom and attached to the soil. The pillory, the gallows, and the whipping-post were the sinister arguments that were employed to obliterate all traces of national culture.

Not only was there a complete arrest in the remarkable literary movement that intervened between the Middle Ages and the beginning of the Thirty Years' War, but most of the literary treasures of the previous centuries were destroyed by the royal edicts of the reactionary Hapsburg rulers. This was done with the notion that the brilliant period of Bohemian existence might be blotted out and forgotten. The book-destroyers that were turned loose in the land burned not only all historical and theological works, but every form of literary composition that

---

[26] Professor Monroe has made numerous pilgrimages to Bohemia and his knowledge of Bohemians is intimate and thorough. He is a "Bohemian by adoption."

might suggest to the Bohemian people their glorious past. One book-destroyer, an Austrian priest, boasted with pride that he had burned 60,000 Bohemian books. Many works were carried by the Bohemian exiles to Saxony, Slovakland, and other countries, and preserved; and these, together with others that escaped the fury of pillaging soldiers during the Thirty Years' War, constitute the fragments out of which the literary history before the seventeenth century must be constructed. But these fragments are little more than the planks of a ship that was wrecked on the ocean of national vicissitude.

The modern Bohemian literary movement dates back only one hundred years. Joseph Dobrovský (1753-1829), the patriarch of Slavic philology, initiated the literary movement at the beginning of the nineteenth century. The few other Bohemian scholars of the day—Jungmann, Palacký, Kollár, Šafařík, and the incomparable publicist Charles Havlíček—lent their services to the rehabilitation of a national language that was long supposed to be dead. The letters of Jungmann give us our most intimate accounts of the struggles of himself and his co-patriots during the early day of the modern Bohemian literary renascence.[27]

During the seventeenth and eighteenth centuries the Austrian Government had penalized the publication of books in the Bohemian language and the teaching of the vernacular in the schools of the kingdom. But in spite of prohibitions of the Hapsburg rulers, the vernacular continued to be spoken in the country districts. This fact facilitated the extraordinary progress made in the fields of poetry, drama, fiction, criticism, and historical works during the last fourscore years. The satirical writings of Jan Neruda, the historical dramas of Alois Jirásek, the rich lyrical poetry of Jaroslav Vrchlický (Frida), the bold imaginative compositions of Julius Zeyer, the modernist poetry of J. S. Machar, the great national epics of Svatopluk Čech, the historical works of Francis Palacký, and the political and sociological writings of Thomas G. Masaryk have made notable contributions to the literary history of modern Bohemia. When one recalls the dearth of literature from Teutonic writers in Austria during the same period, the contrast is marked indeed.

In matters of art also Bohemia was early in the field. The Prague school of painting that came into prominence during the reign of Charles IV. (1316-1378) took favorable rank with similar early art movements in Italy. Painters, sculptors, and architects trained in Bohemia are represented to-day at most of the great cities in Europe where art treasures are preserved. The zealous and promising artistic movement inaugurated in the country by the followers of the Prague school, like most of the other culture movements in the kingdom, was well-nigh extinguished by the attempted Teutonization of the country by the Hapsburg rulers after the fatal Bílá Hora.

The political and literary activity in Bohemia during the opening years of the last century reacted favorably on the art life of the nation. A society of the fine arts, that was distinctly Bohemian and national in character, was organized at Prague in 1848; and this was followed by annual expositions of the chief productions of

---

[27] The story is too long to be told in this connection; and the interested reader is referred to "History of Bohemian Literature," by Count Lützow (London and New York, 1899), and "Bohemia and the Čechs," by Will S. Monroe (Boston and London, 1910).

Bohemian and foreign artists. As an immediate result of these activities, Bohemia produced an astonishingly large number of painters who took high rank in their art, artists of the rare talent of Hellich, Manes, Čermák, Schwaiger, Aleš, Brožík, Mucha, Úprka. In sculpture, too, modern Bohemia has taken a place of distinction in the works of Myslbek, Šimek, Seidan, Sucharda, and Šaloun.

Bohemia's music is probably better known throughout the civilized world than any other branch of her creative art. This is largely due to the universal character of the language of music and to the eminence of her great tone poets, Smetana and Dvořák. Not that the history of music in the country begins with these two modern composers, but because they spoke in such musical forms and with such musical force that they arrested the attention of the world.

We read in the chronicles of the mediæval historians of the rôle played by music in the life of the Bohemian people; and we know that during the Hussite period the Bohemian hymnology attained a degree of excellence that has not been surpassed by later ages. The Bohemian school of music of to-day takes foremost rank among the music schools of modern Europe.

Bohemia's position in the matter of education is likewise distinctive. Education of an elementary and secondary character was general in Bohemia several centuries in advance of Austria and Germany. The University of Prague antedated similar institutions in Germany by more than half a century. John Amos Komenský (known in America and England by the Latinized form of his name, Comenius) was a Bohemian, and in the judgment of competent historians of education he was the real evangelist of modern pedagogy. Most of the school systems of progressive and cultivated European peoples are based directly upon ideas that he formulated.

In the domain of religion and ethics, Bohemia has given the greatest moral reformer of the past five hundred years in Jan Hus, the forerunner of Martin Luther, John Calvin, and William E. Channing. And in Jerome of Prague, the contemporary of Hus, she produced another spiritual leader of great power.

Professor Will S. Monroe.

VI.

THE BOHEMIANS
AND THE SLAVIC REGENERATION.

By Leo Wiener, Professor of Slavic Languages and Literatures
at Harvard University[28]

Bohemia is the westernmost Slavic country and its fortunate geographical position between the West and the East of Europe and half-way between the Slavs of the Balkans and those of the North has in past ages determined its cultural mission, which has been that of mediating between the Latin civilization and the Poles on the one hand and the Byzantine culture and the Russians on the other. Bohemia is the keystone in the Slavic arch. Without it the proto-history of the Eastern nations in Europe has no meaning and no coherency. Unfortunately even the most profound scholars have as yet overlooked the important rôle which Bohemia has played in forwarding that Carolingian civilization which the Visigoths, expelled by the Arabs from Spain and settled by Charlemagne in southern and central France, caused to radiate to the whole Germanic world and, through Bavaria, grafted on the neighboring Čechs.

It is well known that the first Christian activity in Bohemia proceeded from German missionaries, but it is only a recent discovery on the origin of the so-called Gothic Bible which has revealed to me the extraordinary extent of the Visigothic literary and cultural influences upon the Bavarians and the Čechs. In the light of this discovery, which I am now subjecting to a close scrutiny, it appears that a tremendous proportion of the Slavic vocabularies, from Russia to Dalmatia, from Poland to Bulgaria, has been borrowed from the religious works of the Bohemians, of the early period, now entirely lost to science. Bohemia was the intellectual mistress of what may be called the proto-Slavic world. Without Bohemia, the greater part of the Slavic vocabularies remains irreducible as regards origins and distribution, while with the proper appreciation of this country's geographical factor it appears at once that far from standing aloof from the Roman civilization of the early Middle Ages, the Slavs have been equal participants with the Teutons in the benefits of the Visigothic culture, which shows hardly any traces of Teutonism, but a curious mixture of Western Roman, Southern French, and Arabic elements. The linguistically strongest of these is the Arabic, for my discovery goes to show that the so-called Gothic Bible was written only about the year 800 and in Southern France.

It was only in 813 that Charlemagne introduced the Germanic languages to

[28] Professor Wiener is a distinguished Slavic scholar whose latest work, "An Interpretation of the Russian People," has just been published.

the knowledge of the educated, by ordering that homilies should be written in the native dialects. There does not exist the slightest evidence that, with the possible exception of some Gothic tracts, which Bishop Ulphilas is said to have written in the fourth century, the Germans used their native dialects for any literary purposes. There is nothing which we possess in the way of literary documents that dates back of the ninth century, and there is precious little that can with certainty be ascribed to a period previous to the tenth century. Hence it appears that the literary Teutonic activity is very little, if at all, ahead of the distinctively Slavic literary activity, which, so far as we know, begins, at the end of the ninth century, with the translation of the Bible by the proto-apostles of the Slavs, Cyril and Methodius, for the Čechs of Bohemia.

In the present stage of philological science it is impossible to ascertain the precise dialect in which these Bulgarian monks wrote, though the reasonable assumption is that it was that of their native Thessalonica. But the existence of a distinct Slavic alphabet, the Glagolica, of which Cyril's alphabet is but a simplification, and the existence of the Freisingen fragments which, although not older than from the eleventh century, are written in a variant dialect and obviously are based on documents preceding the activity of the proto-apostles, make it certain that Cyril and Methodius drew on an older literary stock or composed in a language which was already permeated by the Christian conceptions which were the common possession of the Čechs in Carolingian times. This is proved by the precious Kiev fragments, of the eleventh century, which contain the most primitive form of the Old-Slavic language and, at the same time, use distinctively Čech words of the Roman Catholic liturgy. It is, therefore, plausible that whatever dialect was later chosen by Cyril and Methodius in their religious activity in Moravia and Bohemia, it was based on the vocabulary which was already familiar to the Čechs from their previous relations with the German missionaries.

The Slavic liturgy did not survive long in Bohemia. After the death of Methodius in 885 the Slavic priests were banished and Moravia and Bohemia became Roman Catholic once more. Only the Abbey of Sázava continued to use the Slavic liturgy until the year 1096, after which nothing more is heard of the Slavic Church. Cyril and Methodius, who had come to Moravia at the request of Prince Rostislav, had in 867 been accused by the German missionaries of heresy, which accusation, however, Pope Hadrian found to be groundless. But the Slavic activity could not be maintained against German arrogance, and, as it was Bishop Wiching who soon after the death of Methodius banished the Slavic liturgy from Bohemia, so it was in the eleventh century again German priests who destroyed the last vestige of the incipient Slavic culture. The Slavic liturgy left the country to become permanently associated with the Greek Catholic Church in Russia, Serbia, and Bulgaria. What might have formed a bond between the various Slavic nations had been senselessly destroyed in Bohemia by the machinations of the German clergy.

Again it was Bohemia which was the first country, not only among the Slavs, but in the whole of Europe, to carry high the banner of religious freedom. The Germans boast of the contribution to freedom of thought by their Luther, and they constantly forget that a century before him Hus had prepared the ground for that religious dissent which was voiced by Luther and his contemporaries. In the fourteenth century Bohemians were fond of attending foreign universities, especially those of Paris and Oxford. In the latter place they became acquainted with Wiclif and, returning home, they translated his works and laid the foundation for that remarkable activity which is known as Husitism. Matěj of Janov, who had studied at Paris, had even before Hus put himself in opposition to Popery, but it was Hus's particular desert to have roused the Čech national feeling. Hus was opposed not only to the corruptions that had crept into the Church, but also to the anti-nationalistic activities of the Germans, and so headed the movement which had for its purpose a Čech regeneration. Čech became the language of intercourse, and a large number of translations of the Bible into Čech was made between 1400 and 1430, the most remarkable being that written by a Taborite miller's wife.

Hus became the first rector of the Čech Prague University, after the German students had withdrawn to the newly formed University of Leipsic. Bohemia was rent by disorder, not only from without, but also within the Husitic movement itself. Husitism stood not only for religious freedom, but also for democracy, and for a time the Husites got along without a king. The most advanced of these democratic protagonists of that time was Chelčický, who dreamed of a millennium, not unlike the one represented in literature at the present time by Tolstoy. His chief desert lies in having, by his writings, promoted the formation of the Church of Bohemian Brethren. The idea of Slavic nationality was not confined to Bohemia alone. The growth of a similar national feeling in Poland may be discerned as the result of this Čech renascence, and the Southern Slavs, too, were directly and indirectly influenced by the nationalism in the North. Indeed, the golden age of Polish and Serbian literature is but a century older than the rebirth of the Slavic idea in Bohemia.

Again it was a Bohemian who, at the end of the eighteenth and in the beginning of the nineteenth century, became the founder of Slavic philology and the new Slavic literary movements throughout Europe. Jagić begins his stupendous "Encyclopedia of Slavic Philology" with a definition of Slavic philology, after which he says: "Only at the end of the eighteenth century did the whole volume of Slavic philology, as an independent science, assume shape. The chief desert in this matter belongs to Joseph Dobrovský. He laid the foundation for a scientific grammar of the Slavic languages, centering it on its most ancient type, the Church-Slavic. He was the first to attempt a determination of the degree of relationship between the separate Slavic dialects by means of a scientific classification. It was he who introduced into the circle of scientific interests the questions from the literary and cultural history of the Slavs, for example, the question of the educational activity of Cyril and Methodius, and finally also from social history, such as archeological and ethnographical questions.... The critical spirit of Dobrovský with his broad views has created Slavic philology. He is the father of this science."

In the second half of the eighteenth century it looked as though the Slavic languages were doomed to perdition. Poland lost its independence and was parceled out among three nations; Bohemia had become a mere dependency of the Hapsburg Empire; Serbia and Bulgaria were under the Turkish yoke and did not even dream of a separate political existence. Nor did matters stand better in the national literatures. The Polish and Bohemian literatures led a vegetative existence; the Serbians and Croatians had forgotten of their literary past; the Bulgarians had not yet discovered the fact that they spoke an intelligible language worthy of literary refinement. Russia was still struggling with the establishment of a linguistic norm out of the ecclesiastic Slavic and the spoken idiom, while its literature was but a feeble reflex of French pseudo-classicism. Nowhere was there the slightest conviction that the homely native dialects had a right to exist by the side of the more fortunate German, while of the past of the Slavic languages but the faintest surmises had been uttered by men untutored in historical and philological lore. But if it was the preponderant influence of German culture that put the Slavic into the shade, it was also the result of German philosophy which gave the Slavic national idea a new lease of life.

German literature had itself been decadent for some time, and was obliged to yield to the more universal French culture which ruled even at the Prussian court. The revolt against French pseudo-classicism and encyclopedism was, however, voiced by a few German writers who began to look in the native elements of the intellectual life for a basis for a native poetry and belles lettres in general. Thus arose the German Romanticism, which believed that in the creations of the popular mind could be found truer, more natural sentiments for literary expression than in the artificial productions of a select upper class. Possibly the chief activity in the direction of a simpler literature was developed by the brothers Grimm, who, by their collections of fairy tales and mythological lore, laid the foundation for a nationalistic movement which was soon to sweep over Europe. Not only did German literature successfully establish itself against the French fashion, but all the smaller nations, who had almost forgotten of their historical existence, began to discover themselves. If the popular creation was truer and more important than the traditional literatures of the Græco-Roman type, then Serbia and Bohemia and Russia, which had preserved an enormous mass of oral literature in out-of-the-way places, harked back to important pasts and should develop from within. The nationalistic idea began to grow out of proportion to the folklore which could conveniently be mustered in proof of native superiority, and where there was such a disproportion it became necessary, so unscrupulous nationalists thought, to manufacture such material. Everybody knows the huge literary forgery of Macpherson, whose Ossianic poetry none the less had a great influence upon susceptible minds, even in the East. Another such forgery was that of the Bohemian Hanka, whose Queen's Court Manuscript still finds overzealous defenders among a certain class of unwise nationalists. It is not the forgery of Hanka which has had most widespread influences upon the dissemination of the nationalistic idea among the Slavs, but the legitimate and scholarly activity of the father of Slavic philology, Joseph Dobrovský.

Having studied Eastern languages at the University of Prague, he had hoped to become a missionary in India, but he soon abandoned this intention and devoted himself to the study of Slavic antiquity. In 1779 he made his appearance in criticism with a periodical which set itself the task of telling "the truth, the naked, unvarnished truth" without regard for persons. He at once attracted attention by his sharp, critical acumen. His main interest lay in the purification of the Čech language and the formation of a literary norm. In 1792 his desire to reconstruct the Slavic past took him on a long journey to the libraries of Sweden and Russia, and even to the Caucasus, where he had expected to find some indications of a Čech origin. In the same year appeared his "History of the Bohemian Language and Literature," in which he described the struggles of the Čech language against the German and Latin from the time of Hus until his day, and showed what relation it bore to the other Slavic languages. The effect of this work upon the nationalistic feeling was very great. Especially his grammar of the Čech language which he published in 1808 formed the basis for all Slavic grammars written in the first half of the nineteenth century. Dobrovský was a voluminous writer, and his scientific correspondence, lately edited by Jagić, contains an immense amount of material which throws a light upon the history of the Slavic renascence.

Dobrovský soon gained many disciples in the Slavic world. The Russians Vostokov, Kalaydovich, Stroev, and many others, the Slovenes Kopitar and Vodník were his followers, and the great Slavists Šafařík and Miklosich carried on the work of philology after him. He enjoyed the friendship of German scholars and poets, Goethe, Jacob Grimm, Pertz, and others. Goethe wrote of him: "Abbé Joseph Dobrovský, the past master of critical historical science in Bohemia, this rare man who long before had followed the general study of the Slavic languages and histories with genial industry and Herodotic travels, rejoiced in reducing his gains to the study of the Bohemian people and country, and thus united with the greatest glory in science the rare reputation of a popular name. The master is visible in whatever he attempts. He everywhere grasps his subject and deftly unites the fragments into one whole."

It cannot be said that the strong nationalistic movement which developed in Bohemia was entirely beneficial, for it not only led to unhealthy, ecstatic moods in the Bohemian literature of the first part of the nineteenth century, but even to a series of literary falsifications which still form the subject of discussion among laymen. But it must not be forgotten that the Bohemian nationalism was a reflex of the nascent German nationalism and was fanned to exaggerated manifestations by the obscurant absolutism of Emperor Francis I. Indeed, the Čech nationalism was to a great extent encouraged by the Austrian Government, as a protective measure against Napoleonic sympathies. The work begun by Dobrovský was carried into the field of literature by Jungmann, who was not satisfied with creating a native literary language for the lower classes only, which seemed sufficient to Dobrovský, but set about to create a literary norm for the whole of the Bohemian people. Jungmann was especially successful in translating from foreign languages, and the Slovaks Šafařík and Kollár, and the Moravian Palacký, not only imitated the activity of their teacher Jungmann, but became even more important in the dissemination of the Slavic idea, both at home and abroad.

In the twenties of the nineteenth century the fame of these ardent Slavists had spread to all the Slavic countries, and in Russia the question of founding a chair of Slavic philology, to be occupied by some Bohemian scholar, was seriously considered. In 1830 the Russian Government offered a chair of Slavic philology to Šafařík, but nothing came of it, chiefly through the machinations of the forger Hanka, who sided with the Russian autocracy, while Šafařík publicly expressed himself in favor of the Poles in the revolution which had just broken out in Russia. But Šafařík continued to exert a great influence on Slavic science in Russia through his friend Pogodin, who never gave up the hope that Šafařík might be called to a chair in Petrograd. When this hope could not be materialized, the young Slavists then studying in Russia, Bodyanski, Sreznevski and others, made it their business to study for a time in Austria, more especially, to meet Šafařík and learn something from personal contact with him. Indeed, the main activity of Bodyanski consisted in translating into Russian the works of Šafařík and other Bohemian Slavists. Similarly Sreznevski, in his inaugural lecture at the university, pointed out the fact that there had existed no interest in Slavic studies in Russia until such had been created by the Bohemian and Serbian scholars. As Bodyanski stood in relation to the Russian Slavophiles, it is certain that the Slavophile movement in Russia received some of its ideas directly or indirectly from the Bohemian nationalists.

From the humble beginnings in the first part of the nineteenth century Bohemian literature has developed in a remarkable manner, borrowing what is best in all literatures, and to a considerable extent falling under the influence of the great Russian writers. It is eminently cosmopolitan in compass and subject-matter, but at the same time has preserved many national characteristics, which would well repay the interest of an English reading public, if it could be induced to read translations of this almost unknown literature. Its poetry is especially attractive and varied, and the poets have reveled in the discussion of those social problems which elsewhere have been relegated to the field of prose.

Whatever the interest of the outsider may be in Bohemian literature, it deserves the highest attention on the part of the Slavs, who owe their very regeneration to the labors of the Bohemian scholars a century ago. If, in addition, we consider what Bohemia did for freedom of religious thought a hundred years before the days of Luther, and still more, the great obligation under which the Greek Catholic Church is to Bohemia for its very ecclesiastic language and national alphabets, the sympathies of the world should particularly be enlisted for this country in the possible future reconstruction of the Austrian Empire. Slavs and non-Slavs should unite on this point without discussion, and even the Germans should look favorably on the restoration of Bohemia to its former freedom and glory, if they are not blinded by selfishness and useless conceit. Bohemia has in the Middle Ages been the mediator between the West and the East, the South and the North, and it will for a long time remain the mediator between the best German thought and the growing Slavic civilization, if the Germans do not, as in the past, rouse the Slavic antipathies. Of all the Slavs, the Bohemians understood the German ideas best, and Dobrovský and other Bohemian Slavists promoted the Slavic idea by means of the German language. That, of course, can never happen again, for the nationalist life is there permanently established. But there is no reason for racial antagonism in a country where Germans and Slavs have lived together for centuries.

PROFESSOR LEO WIENER.

ADDENDA.
THE BOHEMIANS AS IMMIGRANTS.

By Emily Greene Balch, Professor of Economics at Wellesley College[29]

In some cities, as for instance Cedar Rapids, and in some states, as for instance Nebraska, Bohemians are a large enough element in the population to be fairly well known; but they are not so numerous in the United States as a whole, as to be clearly present to the minds of most people. New Yorkers may have seen with interest the National Hall of the Bohemians, Clevelanders may be familiar with the Schauffler Missionary Training School, persons familiar with industrial conditions in Chicago may be aware of the great Bohemian colony there, the largest in the country; but in general if people know anything about Bohemians they probably "know a great many things that aren't so," misled by the fact that the French word for Gipsies is Bohemians, much as our word for the American aborigines is Indian.

Yet from the colonial period individual Bohemians have come to this country, and in 1906, the latest year for which I have estimates, the Bohemian group was put at a round half-million.

Some of these early settlers are picturesque and not unimportant figures like Heřman and Phillipse, but it was not till the disturbed period of 1848 that Bohemians came to this country in appreciable numbers. At this time there was a triple ferment in Bohemia: first, a desire for political independence; second, a resurrection of national self-consciousness symbolized by the revival of the Bohemian language, the use of which among cultivated people had been abandoned for German; and third, a spirit of religious questioning and vehement challenge of current Christianity, largely due to reaction against the influence of a corrupt Austrian clericalism.

Another possible influence was the discovery of gold in California in 1849, which is said to have brought Bohemian gold-seekers and to have stimulated the activity of ship agents. The census of 1850 mentions 87 natives of Austria (out of 946 in the United States) as then in California; these were probably Bohemians. Throughout the fifties and early sixties there was a pretty steady outflow from Bohemia, most of it directed to the United States. This early emigration was a movement of settlers, whole families going together.

With 1867 came a fresh impulse to emigration. Besides the newly granted right to emigrate freely, the disastrous war with Prussia in 1866 gave added reasons for

---

[29] Author of "Our Slavic Fellow-Citizens." Miss Balch studied the Slav in the United States and "at the source," in Europe.

going, while in the United States the Civil War was over and everything invited the settler.

The earliest colony of Bohemians was in St. Louis, where in 1854 they had already established a Catholic church, and this city has always remained an influential Bohemian centre.

More important, however, was the movement to the states further West—the largest numbers settling in Wisconsin, later Iowa, later Nebraska and the two Dakotas, though a considerable settlement also grew up in Cleveland. In general, however, in Ohio, Indiana, and Illinois land was already too dear for the newcomers, and they continually settled further west as the years went on. In the early days they either went overland from the Eastern ports or up the Mississippi River. One of the reasons for so many Bohemians as well as Germans, Scandinavians, Poles, and Belgians being attracted to Wisconsin was undoubtedly the attitude of that state toward immigration. A fact that is easily forgotten in the present state of feeling in regard to immigration is the eager and official solicitation of immigrants that was carried on for years by various states. Wisconsin, like many other states, appointed a Commissioner of Immigration to stimulate the inflow. In 1852 the first man to fill this office reported to the Governor that he had been in New York distributing pamphlets in English, German, Norwegian, and Dutch, describing the resources of the state.

After four years this state canvass for immigrants was suspended for a time, but in 1864 the Wisconsin Legislature memorialized Congress for the passage of national laws to encourage foreign immigration on the ground that labor was scarce, owing to the war, and that wages had more than doubled. Whether or not as a consequence of this request, Congress did in the same year pass an act to encourage immigration, which, however, was repealed in March, 1868.

Again, in 1879, Wisconsin established a State Board of Immigration to increase and stimulate immigration, with authority to disseminate information. The official circulars mentioned as inducements the following points: climate, rich lands at a nominal price, free schools and a free university, equality before the law, religious liberty, no imprisonment for debt, and liberal exemption from seizure by a creditor, suffrage and the right to be elected to any office but that of governor or lieutenant-governor on one year's residence, whether a citizen or not (intention to become one having been declared); and full eligibility to office for all actual citizens. "There is never an election in the state," one circular continues, "that does not put some, and often very many, foreign-born citizens into office. Indeed, there is no such thing as a foreigner in Wisconsin, save in the mere accident of birthplace; for men coming here and entering into the active duties of life identify themselves with the state and her interests, and are to all intents and purposes American." We are told "The language above used is, except in rhetoric, identical" with that in an edition of 1884.

Besides this direct encouragement by the state "a similar canvass was maintained by counties and land companies, and at a later stage by railway companies, some of them sending agents to travel in Europe." Of such solicitation at the very beginning of Bohemian immigration I found tradition still mindful in the old country. Thus immigrants have felt themselves directly and officially invited and urged to come, and it is not surprising that one often finds them aggrieved and hurt at the tone of too many current references making foreigners synonymous with everything that is unwelcome.

Many of the Bohemians were pioneers in the unbroken wilderness, and a very large part were farmers. A large proportion, however, had trades, and this is characteristic of Bohemian immigration in general. The common estimate is that one-half of the Bohemians in the country are living in country places, occupied either with farming or with some one of the various employments incident to rural life, from shoemaking to keeping store or acting as notary public. If the comparison be extended to all groups of foreign parentage, Bohemia shows a larger proportion engaged in agriculture than any foreign countries except Switzerland, Denmark, and Norway, surpassing even Germany and Sweden. It is interesting to note that Italy has a very low rank in this regard; even Poland and Russia surpass her, lowered as their place is by the large non-agricultural Jewish element, and only Hungary is below her.

As to the quality of Slavic farming, one naturally hears different reports. I suspect that the American often thinks the Pole or Bohemian a poor farmer because he works on a different plan, while the foreigner, used to small, intensive farming, thinks Yankees slovenly and wasteful. Especially when he takes up old, worn-out farm lands, he has small respect for the methods of his predecessor, who, he says, "robbed the soil."

The American business agent of a Bohemian farming paper, already quoted, could not say enough in praise of the Bohemian farmers. They farmed better than the Americans. They invested freely in farm machinery. Nothing was too good or too big for them. In the eastern half of Butler County, Nebraska, there were seventeen big steam threshing outfits among Bohemians—something to which you could find nothing parallel in the same area anywhere in the United States. The Bohemian paper of which he was agent had seven times more advertising of farm implements than any other paper in the United States, he said.

While the above statements are those of an interested party, all the available evidence points the same way. It would seem, moreover, as though in certain lines, new to us and familiar in Europe, the immigrant should be able to supply very valuable skill. This seems to be especially the case in the sugar-beet industry, in which the labor of Bohemians, who understand beet culture well, is much sought.

Of Bohemian women at work, nearly a quarter were in 1900 servants and waitresses, and more than another quarter workers at tailoring or in tobacco. This corresponds to the fact that many Bohemians in the cities are engaged in the two latter branches; many too are mechanics or trades-people, often carrying on a small business of their own.

The Bohemians, like other Slavic groups in this country, are much given to organizing into societies. Many of their associations are small local affairs of the most various sorts. In a New York Bohemian paper I found a list of 95 local societies among this group of perhaps 45,000 people. Many were mere "pleasure clubs," to use the current East Side phrase, while many were lodges of various of their great "national" societies. Of these large national societies the most remarkable is the society founded by the Bohemians at St. Louis in 1854, under the name of the Bohemian-Slavonic Benevolent Society, or as it is commonly called, by the initials of this name in the vernacular, the Č. S. P. S. In the religious controversies which soon divided American Bohemians into two camps, this came to represent the free-thinking, anti-Catholic side. It numbers about 25,000 members.

The Sokols, which correspond to the German "Turnerbunds" or gymnastic societies, are as popular and widespread as they are desirable. They give opportunity for exercise dignified by a sense of the relation between good physical condition and readiness for service to one's country. Women and children, as well as the men, have their own divisions, classes, and uniforms, and the Sokol exhibitions are important and very pretty social events. In Prague, in the summer of 1906, the Bohemian Sokols had an anniversary international meet, at which the American societies were also represented, and performed evolutions, literally in their thousands, in the open air.

Theatricals, whether given in some local hall or in a regular theatre hired for the occasion, are, as in Europe, a favorite employment for Sunday afternoons or evenings. Classic pieces, both literary and operatic, are much enjoyed; for instance, among the Bohemians, Smetana's opera, "The Bartered Bride," is often given. On the other hand, one will see a very simple spontaneous little exhibition given with the greatest abandon and delight by a club of hard-worked, elderly women, whose triumphs are hugely enjoyed by their families and neighbors. It is an especial pleasure to them to reproduce the pretty costumes of their old-world youth. Worthy of especial mention are the club called Snaha (Endeavor), of Bohemian professional women in Chicago, and the clubs organized for reading and study among Socialists of different nationalities.

There are numerous Bohemian papers and periodicals, including the Bohemian "Hospodář" ("Farmer") of Omaha and the "Ženské Listy" of Chicago, the latter being an organ of a woman's society, printed as well as edited by women. It is not devoted to "beauty lessons" and "household hints," but to efforts toward woman's suffrage and the "uplifting of the mental attitude of working-women." Its 6,000 subscribers include distinguished Bohemians all over the country, men as well as women.

In religion the Roman Catholics claim a large number of Bohemians, but there is a substantial Protestant minority; outside the church fold is the numerous and very interesting group of Free-Thinkers.

The Bohemians are among the most literate of our immigrants. Taking the data for 1900, which I happen to have worked out, we find that of immigrants of all nationalities of fourteen years and over, those not able to both read and write were 24.2 per cent.; among the Germans 5.8 per cent.; among the Bohemians and Moravians only 3.0 per cent.; among Scandinavians, under 0.8 per cent. Certainly to supply only about one-half as many illiterates per hundred as the Germans is a notable record.

All of this is quite borne out by the impression one gets of Bohemians both in the United States and in Bohemia. In development and conditions they rank with the immigrant from northwestern Europe. The struggle with the Germans is in a sense the master-thread in their whole history, and this contact, even though inimical, has meant interpenetration and rapprochement. No other Slavic nationality is more self-conscious and patriotic, not to say chauvinistic, in its national feeling, and at the same time none begins to be so permeated with general European culture and so advanced economically.

As to character, if it is impossible to indict a whole people, so is it impossible to draw a portrait of such a collective group. Nevertheless, no one can doubt that one characteristic of the countrymen of Smetana and Dvořák is their noble gift for music. Their sense of color, too, is very marked, and they, beyond all people I know, love the dance. Yet with all their "gemüthlich" and temperamental qualities I find them reserved, delicate, shy, intensely family-loving, cherishing privacy.

The Bohemians are a people of high conscientiousness, and by nature loyal. In the Civil War their anti-slavery feeling and their devotion to their new country both were shown, and the first company that went from Chicago to fight for the Union is said to have been a Lincoln Rifle Company that some young men of that nationality had organized in 1860. The dominating feature in the great Bohemian National Cemetery in Chicago is the soldiers' monument, just such a monument as stands on every village common in New England; and perhaps nothing so much as this visible sign of blood shed in the same cause bridges the difference of national feeling.

They are interested in ideas for their own sake, as are the Latin peoples, and especially in questions of religion. The older people love their past, their language, their old home, yet they cannot hand on these interests in their pristine intensity to the younger people, absorbed in the life about them, dropping their Bohemian speech and ways and gradually, only gradually, completing the transition to the New World and its ways.

PROFESSOR EMILY G. BALCH.

NOTE.—I have to thank the publishers of my book, *Our Slavic Fellow-Citizens*, for permission to borrow here and there from its pages.

Lector House believes that a society develops through a two-fold approach of continuous learning and adaptation, which is derived from the study of classic literary works spread across the historic timeline of literature records. Therefore, we aim at reviving, repairing and redeveloping all those inaccessible or damaged but historically as well as culturally important literature across subjects so that the future generations may have an opportunity to study and learn from past works to embark upon a journey of creating a better future.

This book is a result of an effort made by Lector House towards making a contribution to the preservation and repair of original ancient works which might hold historical significance to the approach of continuous learning across subjects.

HAPPY READING & LEARNING!

LECTOR HOUSE LLP
E-MAIL: lectorpublishing@gmail.com

www.ingramcontent.com/pod-product-compliance
Lightning Source LLC
LaVergne TN
LVHW091526170726
843492LV00004B/1080